Heaven Help Us
Short Stories Volume One

by

Dale Roy Erickson

Copyright © 2013 Dale Roy Erickson

ISBN 978-0-988-4145-1-8

All Rights Reserved

Published by Prayerful Publishing Inc., Meridian, Idaho, USA

www.prayerfulpublishing.com

Scripture taken from the NEW AMERICAN STANDARD BIBLE
Copyright c 1960, 1962, 1963, 1968, 1971, 1972, 1973, 1975, 1977, 1995
by The Lockman Foundation Used by permission www.Lockman.org

No part of this publication may be reproduced in any form, stored in any retrieval system, posted on any website, or transmitted in any form or by any means – digital, electronic, scanning, photocopy, recording, or otherwise – without written permission from the author, except for brief quotations printed in reviews and articles.

The persons and events portrayed in this work of fiction are the creations of the authors, and any resemblance to persons living or dead is purely coincidental.

Moraine Lake cover page photo provided and used by permission of Timothy Erickson.

Revised Second Edition

ACKNOWLEDGMENTS

To the only true God and His Son, Jesus, who brings us grace, forgiveness and life; Connie Erickson who has stood with me through all of life's adventures; Danney Clark for his significant contribution to this effort; Larry Patrick for his friendship, insight, encouragement and creative graphics design; the Prayerful Publishing board of directors for their prayers, wisdom and support; Kelly Roberts for her gracious and painstaking editing; and to the host of people who challenged us to keep pressing on to the finish line. It's not over yet and the best is yet to come.

Preface

The short stories of Heaven Help Us Short Stories Volume One can each stand alone and should be appreciated by anyone. They are part of a multi-platform curriculum designed to help young people grow in their connection with God. The short stories volumes one and two are designed to be part of the homework for the curriculum. The 35-lesson curriculum will include 35 short stories, a smartphone application that provides seven thoughts on prayer with the supporting Scripture for each lesson (a total of 245 prompts), an active participation student manual, a teacher's manual with guidelines for teaching the lessons, a session planning sheet for each lesson, additional teacher resources, and of course, tests for each unit.

The curriculum is designed for the following possible settings: release time courses for public schools, middle school and high school youth groups, home school, Christian schools, and the training of indigenous Christian leaders.

Table of Contents

Cathy's Camaro	1
Triggers	10
New Job	22
A Woman's Scream	29
Extraordinary	35
Triumph	40
Reluctant Hero	52
Improvise I	60
Improvise II	77
Fantasies of The Flesh	90
Rewind	112
Significant Works	124
God's Provision	134
Nature Of The Beast	140
Default Line	158
Deception	163
Small Minded	170
It Is Finished	176

Cathy's Camaro

While the offer was less than he wanted, it was more than he expected considering the young man who stood before him.

He went back verbally over the car's amenities one more time, talking mostly to himself but loud enough for the man and his son to hear. His hand gently touched the car from time to time.

"Doesn't use a drop of oil, changed it myself every 2,500 miles. It has never been wrecked ...," he reminded them as the litany of its attributes came to mind. "Did I tell you I have the original rims and hubcaps in the garage?"

Of course he had told them, more than once, how he and his wife had bought the car new back in '68 – their first new car. That the car did not drip or leak fluids was evidenced by the lack of stains on the concrete beneath it.

"Original paint, I've kept it garaged the whole time, not a tear in the seats either," he reminded the prospective buyers. "I bought the chrome rims for my wife's birthday," he added, "it was her car."

"It's beautiful," the young man said. "I love it."

Ben turned toward the father who stood quietly behind his son. "It's a 396 with a four barrel carb you know, lots of horsepower for a young man to control," he warned. "Do you think he's up to that?"

The father smiled as he looked at his 17-year-old son. "If he can't it will be parked until he can, or it will be sold. First ticket, it goes on the shelf for a month, second he loses the keys for a year."

Ben nodded. He liked both the boy and his father.

Truth be told, he'd have given the car to the boy, but a gift does not hold the same value as something that is earned.

"Whose money are we talking about here?" he asked as though he had the right to know. "Yours or his?"

"Mine, sir," the boy answered. "I earned it myself mowing lawns the last two summers."

Ben liked the way the sandy-haired young man addressed him, calling him sir, with respect evident in his voice. He also liked his deportment and how he had obviously resisted society's fashion trends by dressing in clean clothes that fit rather than baggy pants, which rode below the butt.

"I've had collectors offer me twice as much," Ben said pausing for effect, "but I couldn't bear the thought of some rich guy trashing Cathy's car or buying it to sell for a profit."

In the few seconds that followed, Ben could tell the boy was prepared to accept rejection or an impossible counteroffer. After a reasonable amount of time had passed he said, "Tell you what, I'll take your money and put it in my bank. You mow my lawn through the summer, and if I see you have taken good care of the car, I'll pay you for your work and you keep the car. If not, I'll give you your money back, take back the title, and you've worked all summer for nothing. Agreed?"

Out of the corner of his eye Ben could see that the father was smiling. However, he did not say a word, choosing rather to leave the negotiations to his son.

The young man hesitated for only a moment and then said, "That sounds more than fair to me. I'll mow it for free."

"No," Ben insisted, "I'll pay you twenty-five dollars a week, but hold the money for you until the end of the summer. A man is entitled to get paid for his work."

The father made eye contact with Ben, gave him a nod of respect, and then accepted an enthusiastic hug from his son.

"Come inside," Ben offered. "I'll get the title and draw up the paperwork so that we are all in agreement as to the terms."

As they sat together sharing soft drinks, Ben signed off on the title and moved his name into the space reserved for lien holder. He explained to Thomas, his young buyer, that the money would be held in an escrow account, which would not be accessed until the full terms of the agreement were satisfied. He kept his eye on the father who sat quietly nodding his affirmation as Ben made each point. When things were settled Tom said, "Dad, this is the answer to my dreams. I've been praying about a car like this for years."

An hour later they left, Tom driving the Camaro and his father following behind in his pickup laden with spare rims, tires, oil filters, extra shocks and other sundry parts.

Ben felt a sadness he could not explain, not over the car per se, but because it represented the last of the physical ties he had with his wife. After she had passed there had been a time when he could not bear to part with a single object that her hand had touched. Some of her things seemed to almost gain a reverence in his mind, things like a hairbrush, a robe, even her eyeglasses were elevated to a sacred and irreplaceable place. Little by little, day by day, God gave Ben a sense of peace and comfort that allowed him to part with them. Cathy's Camaro represented the last of the earthly things she had treasured and enjoyed before she had been taken home.

~ ~

In early spring, when the daffodils and crocus had pushed their heads above ground, Ben saw the Camaro pull into his driveway. It had been several months since the car had been sold, but he had made no attempt to contact the boy trusting in their handshake agreement.

"Morning, Mr. Brown," he said with a smile as he walked up the driveway. "I thought I should come by and work out the details with you before the weeds begin to take over. Seems like one day there aren't any, the next they've taken over everything."

"Right you are," Ben agreed. "God gives them a little sun and a little rain and they take right off. Please call me Ben," he added.

Although Tom was still a little nervous he stepped away from the car and said, "Do you want me to use your mower or mine?"

"Mine already knows the yard. No sense in you having to load and unload yours," Ben answered. "And I have the trimmer and gas here as well."

Tom nodded then asked, "Is Saturday alright? I am still in school until the end of May, and then I can mow anytime of the week."

Ben nodded. "Saturday is fine. Let me show you where I keep things just in case you come by when I'm not home."

They walked behind the house and stopped at a small garden shed where Ben worked the combination lock until it opened.

"Let me show you where I have written the combination down," Ben said smiling. "Sometimes I get out here and forget it myself."

He showed Tom the secret spot where he had hidden the numbers that opened the door and began to explain its contents.

"Mower takes regular gas. The can is right here. Push the primer bulb five times and it starts on the first or second pull. Same with the weed whacker up here," he said, pointing to where it hung on the wall. The shelves neatly displayed the various weed killers, fertilizers, trash bags, gloves and miscellaneous paraphernalia that one accumulates as a homeowner.

Tom nodded as he looked over the equipment. "Can I get a start on the flowerbeds while I'm here?" he asked.

Ben nodded, appreciating the boy's eagerness. "How about after lunch?" he said. "I was just about ready to sit down to a little soup and a sandwich. I'd enjoy the company."

That is how their relationship began. It became a regular thing to see Tom show up in the old Camaro just before lunchtime every Saturday, a smile on his face, and a teenage appetite waiting to be satisfied. *The car looks spotless, show room new*, he thought to himself whenever Tom pulled up.

~ ~

"How's she running?" Ben asked one day. "Havin' any problems with her?"

"Pings sometimes if I take off too hard. I can't seem to figure it out," Tom said between bites.

"Octane," Ben announced proudly. "She's a muscle car designed for 100+ octane. You can't buy the good gas anymore so you have to compensate by resetting the timing."

"I set it to specs the first time I tuned it up," Tom responded.

"There's the problem," Ben offered. "I had it slightly retarded so it wouldn't ping using the low-quality gas."

Ben enjoyed the fact that he could share his limited knowledge with someone by teaching his young friend what he knew.

"Try four degrees advanced at an idle and see how she responds. Or, buy some octane boost," Ben suggested.

"Thanks, I will," Tom answered enthusiastically. "The guy at the tire store told me I need upper ball joints. He showed me how loose they were while he was rotating the tires."

Ben smiled. "Don't believe him," he said. "It's just an unscrupulous sales trick to sell you something you don't need. The only way to measure wear in the ball joints is with the springs depressed. You can't do that while it is on the rack."

Ben could tell that the boy was evaluating what he had said. "Look at the maintenance book in the glove box and you'll see the mileage when they were replaced," Ben added. "Same thing with the shocks, belts and fluids."

~ ~

Summer finally arrived, school was out, and the sun had done its magic on every living thing. God's plan was working perfectly causing plants, including the grass, to grow and prosper. Ben liked to putter around the yard and enjoyed Tom's visits, even though he did not really need the assistance. He was careful to allow the boy enough to do while he busied himself planting, fertilizing and watering. After the mowing and trimming were done Tom would often stay over for a time just to visit. He would share his aspirations and plans for the future with Ben.

"How are your grades?" Ben asked, feeling their friendship had given him license to inquire.

"A's and B's," Tom answered without hesitation. "But I struggled in math this year. We had a new teacher in the last quarter."

"It can be tough getting in sync with change," Ben admitted. "Sometimes it's the perspective that is the problem. No two teachers come at it the same way even when they are teaching the same topics."

Tom nodded.

"I taught for thirty-two years," Ben said. "I wasn't the same teacher at the end that I was in the beginning."

"Better or worse?" Tom asked laughing.

"Some of each, I expect," Ben admitted. "It kind of balances out. When our stamina and enthusiasm begin to fade with age, our experience, patience, and wisdom are supposed to kick in."

"Why'd you quit?"

"Cathy got sick and needed me more than the students," Ben said, remembering the final years.

Tom nodded. His mouth was full of bologna sandwich.

"You plannin' on going to college?" Ben asked.

"Hope to," Tom answered. "But things aren't looking too good right now."

"How so?" Ben asked.

"Dad's had his hours cut back at the shop, and my mom's having trouble finding a job. My grades aren't good enough to get a scholarship so I might need to lay off a year and save up my money."

Ben nodded. "Times are tough for a lot of folks right now. What does your father do?"

"He works at a cabinet shop and makes a little furniture on the side. But since the construction slowed down they aren't able to keep all their men busy."

"What are you thinking you will focus on in college?" Ben asked, pouring them each a glass of milk.

"Engineering."

"You'll need good math skills for sure. Maybe I can offer a little help here and there when school starts back up."

The boy looked at him appraisingly, then said, "I'd like that. Do you go to church?"

The question caught Ben off guard. "We used to," he finally said. "Cathy and I went together for years, but I kind of lost interest after she passed."

Tom didn't respond immediately but when he did he got Ben's attention. "I felt the same way when my sister died. I was so angry at God I couldn't stand to be around other Christians. They were always saying nice, little things that were supposed to make me feel better but none of them ever did."

Ben could feel the emotion return as Tom relived the tragedy. "How do you feel about it now?" Ben asked.

"I still miss her," he answered. "I finally got over blaming God for every bad thing that happens. Instead I try and remember to thank Him for every good thing that happens."

Ben nodded, looking at this young man in a different light. "Why did you ask me about church?" he said.

Tom smiled, "You've helped me a lot," he said. "I thought maybe you'd go with us someday and let God help you find some peace."

Triggers

There are some things that just seem to make other things happen ... catalysts ... triggers.

It was not a single event, but several events that placed the wheels in motion. Unknown to them at the time, things were beginning to happen that had been in the works for many years. As surely as the sun rises and sets and rivers flow to the sea, those events preordained by God will come to fruition.

Sarah, not the Sarah of biblical times, but Sarah Angelina Smith, daughter of Michael and Molly Smith of Hartford, Connecticut, unknowingly had an important part to play in God's master plan. Sarah by all accounts was a healthy, happy, 16-year-old from a good Christian home with better than average grades and looks. She was not an exceptional athlete or scholar, but she was honest and trustworthy. That is the main reason her parents, with much trepidation, had allowed her to take driver's training. When she successfully completed the training she immediately pressed for permission to apply for her beginner's license.

But the full-license carrot still hung before her, allowing them in some ways to maintain control over her actions. There were rules and stipulations to her access of the family cars. The watchful eyes of her younger brother recorded each event. They would be recounted in specific detail when his time to drive would come. Siblings only want to be treated as individuals when it benefits them and their cause. The remainder of the time they use the decisions and/or mistakes of the parents with the older children as tickets to be cashed in for personal advantage.

Jacob at thirteen was already feeling the changes that nature was making in both his body and mind. He felt as if he would never be able to catch up to his sister and resented the way his big sister felt the freedom to control his life whenever his dad and mom were out of the house. Now she had access to the car, which was just another of his dreams that she was able to live out before his eyes. One day he was going to prove that he could pass her on the road of life.

Mike was a veteran fireman with ten years of service. Molly was a third-grade schoolteacher. Until recently, life for the family of four had been predictable and comfortable. In three years, Mike would celebrate his fortieth birthday and had already noticed the extra effort it took to keep up with the younger men on his crew. Experience and common sense leveled the playing field in all but the most physical of activities. The daily exercise regimen that had been part of his professional life had now become a real necessity.

The family was sitting at the dinner table finishing up their meal.

"Dad," Jacob said, "what would you think if I got a job?" In his mind he had already picked out the future means of transportation that his paychecks could bring.

Without waiting for her husband to answer, Molly interjected her opinion. "You have a job. It is your job to keep your grades up so that you can get a scholarship for college."

Mike hesitated, letting his wife's advice settle a little before he answered his son. "Just what did you have in mind, son?"

"Well, maybe something like the car wash or a grocery store job. I was thinking of something after school or on weekends, just some way to earn a few bucks," Jacob answered.

"Give your mom and me time to discuss it, and we'll get back to you," Mike said. "But nothing you can do is more important than your education."

He looked at his wife hoping that his last sentence had calmed her fears and would give her reason to consider her son's request. Mike had grown up in a rural setting and had worked at one thing or another since the age of twelve. He felt that it was important that his son learn the value of providing for himself and would share those feelings with Molly at another time.

"How's he supposed to get to work?" Sarah asked. "I suppose that I could give him a ride once I get my full driver's license." Sarah was looking for any opportunity to get access to the car, even if it meant giving her annoying brother a ride.

Both of them wanted to ignore the question, knowing that this was a lose-lose situation.

"Study the driver's manual, pass the written and driving test, show us that you are responsible, and we'll consider it," her mother answered.

Mike nodded, then smiled, knowing that he wouldn't have been as patient or reasonable had he answered her.

"Movie night?" Mike asked his family.

"Yeah!" came the immediate reply, followed quickly by their individual requests, none of which were compatible.

"Okay," he said, "everyone write down your two top picks. We'll throw them in the hat and choose two to watch tonight."

Eight titles went into Molly's mixing bowl. The two winning titles accompanied Mike and Sarah to the video store a few minutes later. Sarah was quick to jump into the driver's seat while her dad settled into the shotgun seat without showing the anxiety he was actually feeling.

Thank God the car insurance is paid and I am surrounded by air bags, he thought.

While they were gone Molly and Jacob put the dirty dishes in the dishwasher and fired up the popcorn popper.

That's unusual. This place is normally packed, Mike thought as he opened the door and entered the giant video store.

At six o' clock on a Thursday night customers were often lined up waiting to pay at both registers. Tonight neither register was manned and no patrons were visible. Mike followed Sarah as she approached the drama movie aisle, intending to move to the section where the action movies were shelved.

He had only gone a few steps when the overhead lights went out. As the lights were replaced by battery-powered emergency lights, Mike and

Sarah tried to acclimate to the darkness. At first, he assumed that there had been a power outage, but looking out he could see the other stores in the area were still lighted. As he was looking, a figure moved toward the front of the store and locked both doors. Sarah was about to yell and announce their presence when Mike put his finger to her lips and crouched between the aisles.

As the footsteps receded toward the stockroom at the rear, Mike whispered, "Something is going on here and I don't think it is good."

"Like what?" Sarah asked.

"Like a robbery or worse," her father answered, taking his cell phone from his pocket.

"911 emergency," came the nearly immediate response. "What is the nature of your emergency?"

"This is Lieutenant Mike Smith of the Hartford Fire Department," Mike said speaking softly. "I am at the video store on South Maple, which I believe is being robbed."

"Can you see inside?" she asked. "Are there citizens in danger? Are there any injuries?"

"My daughter and I are inside the store. Someone has turned out the lights and locked the doors. They are unaware of our presence," Mike answered. "We do not know the number of people inside or their intent. Everyone seems to be in the back part of the building."

"I'll notify the police and ask them to send someone right out," she said.

"Ask them to keep it low key, no lights or sirens," Mike said. "They may have hostages."

"I'll pass on your suggestion," she said.

"I'm putting my phone on vibrate," Mike said. "Call me back if necessary."

Sarah's eyes were big. Even in the darkness Mike could tell his daughter was frightened.

From their position they could hear several voices talking in muted tones and the sound of someone crying. It was nearly 100 feet from where they were to the front doors and almost as far to the voices.

Mike was thanking God that he had not brought the whole family and praying at the same time for His protection.

"What do we do?" Sarah asked. "Do we just wait until the cops arrive? What if they hurt someone?"

Mike had already been considering what measures seemed prudent. "I think it makes sense to try and find out more of what is going on back there without alerting them," he answered. "Then we can give the cops a heads up."

Sarah nodded.

"You stay here with the phone and take any calls that come in. I'll get a little closer and see what I can find out. It's risky to move around too much, too easy to knock something over or make noise." Mike said. "Try and stay where I can find you."

Again Sarah nodded, then said, "Dad, be careful."

Mike smiled and nodded back. "Count on it," he answered.

~ ~

"Police dispatch. What is the nature of the emergency?" came the response to the 911 operator's call.

"I have a reported Code 3, robbery in progress, at the video store on South Maple. We have identified two friendlies inside who are presently unknown to the perps: a fireman and his daughter."

"Hostages?" the dispatcher asked.

"Unknown," the 911 operator responded. "We were asked to approach without lights and sirens."

Two undercovers, a black and white and an ambulance were on the scene in four minutes. The patrol car took up a position at the rear of the store, the unmarked cars were in the lot among other parked vehicles, while the ambulance stayed out of sight.

The phone in Sarah's pocket vibrated. She answered it quietly.

"What's taking so long?" Jacob asked. "Mom and I have already eaten almost all of the popcorn."

"Put Mom on," Sarah ordered.

Jacob did not see the necessity. "Just tell me," he argued.

"Put her on now," she answered, trying to make her point without raising her voice.

Jacob tried to argue a second time, but Sarah had hung up.

It was Molly who called back. "What's going on?" she asked. "Why are you and Dad taking so long?"

"Mom," she said, "we are locked inside the store. Dad thinks it's being held up. He's gone to try and find out. The police are on their way."

It took several seconds for her words to make sense to Molly. "Can't you just get to the doors and get out?" she finally asked.

"They locked it with a key," Sarah said. "We watched them."

Cold fingers of fear caressed Molly's heart as she pictured the scene. Satan magnified her fear with an image of her husband and daughter lying on the floor bleeding. She began to cry.

"Don't cry Mom," came Sarah's voice over the phone. "Just pray for us. We'll be fine."

~ ~

"Get him on the phone," the sergeant said. "Let's see if we can figure out what we're dealing with here."

The phone vibrated again in Sarah's pocket.

"Hello," she said softly, half expecting her mother again.

"This is Sergeant Davidson," the voice said. "Is Mike Smith there?"

"This is his daughter. My dad has gone to the back of the store to find out what's going on."

"Can you hear them?" the sergeant asked.

"Sometimes I can hear them talking, but most of it was just too low for me to understand."

"Do you know how many there are?"

"We only saw the one. The one who locked the front doors before the lights went out," Sarah said. "But from the sounds we can hear from the back room, he clearly is not alone."

"Okay, stay out of sight and have your father give me a call when he gets back," he said.

~ ~

"Get the store manager on the phone," Sergeant Davidson said to dispatch. "I want to know how many employees were scheduled to work tonight. And tell me everything you know about fireman Mike Smith."

A few minutes later dispatch called back. "The manager says there could be as many as three, two for sure. A new part timer was to have joined the two regulars at six, about the time the lights went out."

"Roger that. Two, possibly three," the sergeant confirmed. "What about Smith?"

"Smith is a ten-year fire department veteran, carries the rank of lieutenant, family man with a clean record," she answered. "He served in Afghanistan during the Bush administration, decorated for bravery."

Davidson smiled. "He sounds like a good man to have on the inside," he said to himself and the dispatcher.

Mike had left Sarah only a few minutes before, but it seemed like hours. He was moving slowly, by instinct as much as by sight in the dimly lighted store, being careful not to touch anything that would give him away. As he neared the storeroom, light illuminated the two swinging doors that were meant to restrict the backroom from public view. Someone had left a bucket and mop beside the door, which nearly caused him to stumble and sound an alarm.

Mike could hear the voices of two men distinctly, one sounding older than the other, and the sobbing of a third person, maybe a girl. He searched his pockets for something he could use as an improvised weapon, but came up empty. He removed the mop from the bucket with utmost care and leaned it back against the wall. It was a heavy, commercial-grade mop with both a substantial handle and head. The bucket was nearly full of soapy water.

Carefully he dropped to his knees and moved toward the doorway. Quietly he looked into the lighted room beyond. On the floor were a young man and woman. Their hands and feet were bound, and their mouths were covered with duct tape. Above them stood an older man holding a revolver. Beside him was a younger man without a weapon. They seemed to be arguing about the need to shoot the hostages before leaving. The younger man wanted to leave them bound but alive, and the other was explaining the need to leave no witnesses behind to identify them.

Mike knew he needed to act. There was no time to return to the phone and explain the situation. A decision was about to be made and the man with the gun would be making it. As Mike backed away from the door he nearly tripped over his daughter.

"Sorry, Dad. I got worried about you," Sarah whispered. The police are outside waiting for your report."

"I want you to go over to the next aisle and call the police back. Wait with the line open. Tell them to breach the front door when I yell. Do you understand?" Mike whispered.

Sarah nodded and began to move slowly away.

Carefully Mike lifted the mop bucket and poured the water on the floor in front of the door. In a single motion he threw the bucket as far as he could toward the front of the store and grabbed the mop in both hands.

When the bucket hit, the room was filled with the sounds of falling merchandise. Within seconds the door opened and the two men ran out into the darkness. Mike did not hesitate. He used the heavy handle to smash the older man's wrist, causing the gun to clatter to the floor. The younger man turned toward him in time to accept the blunt end in his rib cage, which knocked the breath out of him.

"Now!" Mike yelled. "Tell them to come in."

The older man attempted to run, but slipped and fell in the soapy water as Mike gave him a substantial rap on the head with the mop. The younger one remained on the floor silent and unmoving. Sarah raced past him and into the storeroom where the two employees lay. She immediately began unbinding them.

"Get the lights," Mike ordered, just as the glass doors shattered.

At the clerk's direction Sarah found the panel that operated the lights and tripped the switch. The room was immediately bathed in light.

"Police! Put your hands in the air!" came the order from the approaching team of policemen.

Mike didn't attempt to argue. Dropping the mop at his feet and placing his hands behind his head, he said, "I'm Mike Smith."

"Pleased to meet you, Mr. Smith," came the quick reply. "I'm Sergeant Davidson. I assume these two men are the would-be robbers," he added, motioning to the two men on the floor.

Just then Sarah and the two employees entered from the storeroom.

"This is my daughter Sarah," Mike said proudly, pointing to Sarah.

The sergeant nodded then asked, "Is everyone all right?"

The older man and his young accomplice were handcuffed and taken into custody while Davidson started gathering information from the four who remained.

"Do you know the men?" he asked the two employees.

"The young guy is Greg," the young woman offered. "Tonight was his first night on the job. He was going to work with us part time. The man with the gun came in right after him and waited until there were no other customers and then took both of us in the storeroom and tied us up."

"They were working together then?" the sergeant asked.

"Yes," the young man replied. "They called each other by name, but the older guy was in charge."

"Did they get any money?"

"Just what was in the two cash registers," he answered. "We can't open the floor safe. Only the manager has the combination."

Sergeant Davidson nodded. "That reminds me," he said, turning to one of the officers standing nearby, "the manager is waiting outside. Will you ask him to join us?" Turning to Mike he said, "Mr. Smith, while we don't usually recommend that citizens take matters in their own hands, we appreciate your timely intervention. You very likely saved lives in doing so. Did your military service prepare you for such emergencies?"

Mike smiled, then answered, "It certainly did. I was a chaplain for three years. I learned that when God puts you in a place He has planned for you, you follow the Lord's direction and wait for Him to pull the trigger."

New Job

Having walked several blocks to the intersection of Grace and 1st streets, I arrived early at my new place of employment. I was determined to make a good first impression.

Although the business had been around for decades, the sturdy building in which it operated belied its age. Like most employers they had allowed me to apply online. However, much to my surprise, they hired me without even a face-to-face interview. My first day on the job would also be the first time I had entered the building.

I entered through a magnificent set of 12-foot solid glass doors with bronze fittings. The lobby was grand in size and furnished in an impressive fashion. The marble floor shone brightly as did the smile on the lips of the young woman at the reception desk. When I offered my best "good morning" she smiled and responded in kind.

"I'm ...," I said, starting to announce myself.

"You are Mr. Shane Cook. We are so glad to see you, Mr. Cook. Please let me show you to the executive offices."

Slightly taken aback by her knowledge and more so by the casual manner in which the business seemed to operate, I smiled and responded, "Thank you."

The nameplate on the gilded desk read Mike Gabriel. The man behind the desk rose and greeted me as we entered.

"Mr. Cook, we have been awaiting your arrival," he said in a friendly tone. Extending his big hand and smiling, he said, "I'm pleased to finally meet you."

Behind him I could see a stunning entryway to the inner offices. The columns on each side of the balconies were polished to the point of reflection, making them seem almost translucent. Below the balconies there was a beautiful white grand piano.

"I hope that my being a few minutes early is not an inconvenience to you."

"Quite the opposite, you arrived just as we expected, prompt to the minute," he said with a reassuring smile. "Do you have any questions about the job before I show you to Mr. Iam's office?"

I had assumed, quite in error, that I had just met the boss. "Only one thing, the actual salary was not mentioned. It just said whatever is fair."

They were both smiling as though they had anticipated my comment.

"As you'll find, Mr. Cook, we operate in what most have come to call a very nontraditional manner. You'll be rewarded for what we are able to accomplish together. If you fail then we will have failed. We want you to give us your very best. You will not be judged by others' opinions of your accomplishment or lack thereof."

Although he hadn't directly answered my questions, I felt comfortable with what he had said.

Try if you can to remember the moment of your birth: the excitement, the pain, and the newness of it all. In a moment, all that you had known for nine months, the familiar comfortable surroundings were gone and a whole strange new world welcomed you. Does a baby have memory of the womb, and if so does it try and hold onto it as life begins anew? It feels now like dozing off during a movie only to awaken and to fall back to sleep again and again. When you are finally fully awake it is difficult to separate the events of your dreams from those of the movie. A gray fog blends the edges of your consciousness into the background until it seems both indistinct and unimportant.

I am trying my best to describe for you how life was before I began my new job. I am not quite sure if it is that I cannot recall, or have no real desire to recall, life as it was.

~ ~

I have been here now for what seems like an eternity at a job I find rewarding and meaningful. The job, about which I once worried, has become second nature just as though it had been especially designed for me. Like others, I will live on site, with all of my needs being met. I will lack nothing and want for nothing. Mr. Gabriel had been correct about the compensation plan, "whatever is fair," I have found is more than I ever could have expected.

The atmosphere within the walls of the business and in the hearts of the employees is best described as harmonious. I've never heard a dispute or an argument, never a look of sadness or discontent.

I'd been filled with questions at first, most of which seem foolish to me now. How long have you been in business? How many people work here? Are you on the DOW Jones Industrials? What guarantees do you have for our futures? Who backs the 401(k)? My questions were foolish, yes foolish and clearly unnecessary, but when I asked I never received any direct answers. By the time I had the answers they were no longer important to me.

Mr. Iam had a presence about him that filled his massive office. He did not speak loudly but was easily heard and understood when he welcomed me as one would greet an old and dear friend.

"Please do come in, Mr. Cook," he said graciously. "We are so pleased you have chosen to join us. I expect our relationship will be a long and fruitful one."

I stood in awe of how this powerful man seemed so humble and in control at the same time.

"Every communication, incoming or outgoing, goes through this office," he said. "I handle each one personally. Nothing, I repeat, nothing is too big or too small that I do not have time to consider and answer it."

I remember wondering if this were some kind of a pitch or something. The idea that the number one man would personally attend to every detail without exception did not seem possible. I wondered what the rest of the staff did.

"What will I be doing?" I asked.

He pointed to two baskets on his desk filled with papers: one labeled incoming, the other outgoing.

"You'll bring me every incoming communication, and then you'll take the outgoing to Mr. Gabriel who will make sure that they are properly handled either by me or one of our staff."

"What are the hours?" I asked next. "When do I begin delivering the correspondence?"

"As soon as you receive them," he answered. "The hour is unimportant. Let me make the decision as to when and how they are answered. You'll be expected to live on site. My son has prepared a place for you. I guarantee you'll like it."

I remember feeling a little uncomfortable, almost captive, wondering if I had gotten myself into trouble. I hesitated knowing that I'd already committed myself to the job, but was fearful just the same.

"When do we get paid?" I asked, immediately regretting how it sounded.

He smiled, and I swear the room lit up.

"Continuously, this is an earn as you go business with a big bonus in the near future," he said excitedly. "Sometimes I pay in advance knowing that you are doing the job willingly."

"You know that I have no experience in this field don't you?" I said half expecting that I'd been hired by mistake.

"I do," he said, smiling again. "But you'll be surprised to find that what you have previously learned will help you do your job here. If you have questions just knock on the door. It is always unlocked."

"Where do I pick up the correspondence that I bring to you? Do we have a mail room?"

"We have a messenger who collects, translates and prepares everything for me. Mr. Gabriel will introduce you to him," he said. "You'll work with him but report directly to me."

I remember feeling guilty for taking up so much of his time, observing that he had mounds of work on his desk and assuming that there would be more on the way.

"I am taking up too much of your time," I said sincerely. "I know you are busy."

Again he smiled. "I always have time for you," he said. "My son calls me the ultimate multitasker."

The job is everything to me now. The past seems to hold less and less interest, while the present blooms with promise and reward. On those rare occasions when I attempt to remember my previous life, the memory of what it was seems like wisps of smoke, intangible and without substance.

Not choosing to stand on ceremony or requiring deferential treatment, the messenger prefers to just be called by his nickname, H.S. He appears to be even busier than Mr. Iam, receiving, translating, and organizing all incoming communication, which in turn is handed off to the boss.

Some have suggested that he can read minds. I don't know about that, but I do know he can speak a thousand languages fluently. He was very helpful to me. It is as though he was my helper rather than the other way around.

Have I mentioned Iam's son? He also goes by his initials, J.C. Everyone can clearly see that he is an in charge kind of guy. He doesn't seem to like it when folks make a big fuss over him. You'd never know by looking at him that he holds a one-third interest in the firm.

He seems to spend most of his time recruiting and hiring new help, then making sure they are comfortable and cared for when they take the job. He always seems to have time for anyone in need or has questions or problems.

He and I have become close friends and spend a fair amount of time together. I heard just today that he is getting married soon. I'm pretty sure we'll all be invited to the ceremony. Word is that it will be one of those events that you won't want to miss and will never forget. I am told the company has unlimited growth potential and is actively seeking new employees. No experience is necessary. I hope you'll consider applying soon.

A Woman's Scream

It was not the piercing sound of an animal in pain that signaled her final escape from this world. Nor could it have been said that it had been an unexpected event. She, like many others before her, had been born to die.

Soma knew from stories told around the campfires that she was a fourth-generation American. Her great-great-grandfather had arrived on a slave ship in the 1700s and had been sold immediately because of his age and size.

Unknown to many, it was not the white man who first began the slave trade. It was the native Africans themselves. Slavery could be dated back for centuries. When one nation conquered another the defeated became the slaves and servants of the victor.

Some masters were cruel and inhumane while others were at least concerned about the welfare of their property. That has been the way of all mankind since time began.

Soma, unlike her father and mother, could read and write quite well. Often they would ask her to read from a tattered old Bible by the firelight. In particular she liked to read the stories of Daniel and Joseph. Both were slaves; but also servants of God who were blessed and revered by their peers and captors alike.

She pictured herself someday being blessed by God to do His work, and like Daniel, valuable beyond what her meager physical skills could boast. She hoped (indeed she often prayed) that God would use her to accomplish great things among her people.

She was six when she started working the fields. At age ten she began serving Lillian in the "big house" of "the massa." Soma's mother had been the nanny for Lillian's daughter, Claire, and had responsibility for her and many of the household chores. Soma learned to read by listening as Claire was given instruction. They had grown up together and initially were as close as sisters, sharing secrets and giggles out of the earshot of their parents. As puberty loomed before them, the fact that Claire was blonde and fair while Soma was tall and black made their differences very evident.

There was a "stir about" among the ranks of the "darkies," as they were called by the white folk. There was discontent, not just among those who were mistreated, but also among those who, like her, were well cared for. Of course many, like her master, had no idea of the cause or the remedy. He looked upon them as ungrateful for his past kindness toward them. As those feelings grew in the minds of the masters they became less sensitive and caring. The slaves noticed the changes and felt all the more unappreciated and devalued. Satan fanned the flames of discontent until the most honest and faithful of the slaves became bitter and stubborn, and their masters more greedy and vengeful.

Back at the turn of the century America was struggling with its newfound independence. The rift between slaves and their masters was growing daily. Someone coined the phrase "whip 'em into shape," as fewer and fewer of the old guard masters found it practical or even possible to control their slaves with kindness.

Soma could still feel the sting when her lifelong friend called her nigger and referred to her as an ungrateful darkie. Claire went off to finishing school without so much as a word or a wave. That winter, a particularly bitter one, they lacked wood to heat their shacks. They were denied axes and horses to gather wood because of their master's fear of an uprising or revolt. Both the whites and blacks were filled with suspicion and pain.

Soma's mother took ill and just before Christmas passed into the waiting arms of Jesus, leaving Soma's father an empty shell of a man. Three of Soma's six brothers were sold and one ran away, leaving the farm without enough hands to do the work when spring finally did arrive. There were eleven laborers now where there had been twenty. Longer hours and shorter breaks were demanded to bring in the cotton and tobacco crops. Where her father used to run the farm with a gentle touch for the massa, now a white overseer with a whip and short temper took his place.

When she was sixteen she began to write in the journal Lillian had given her. She wanted to record her thoughts and feelings when she read the Bible. She took solace in the fact that the Bible spoke of others who had found freedom in Jesus while still in captivity. She read to her father from some of Paul's letters that were written from prison. She explained how she had found salvation and peace by promising herself to Jesus. But her father was bitter and broken, blaming God for taking his wife and not removing the yoke of oppression from their necks. He wasn't ready to hear about a loving God who would let such injustice continue. To him, "all things in God's time" sounded trite when he was struggling every day just to survive, each day full of want with no end in sight.

Soma read over and over about how God's people cried out to Him and He heard their cries and rescued them. She also made note that these things were not changed overnight. Sometimes many years went by before He acted to save His people. It was hard for her to understand, and even more difficult for her to explain, why God seemed to be ignoring their misery.

To compound the farm's problems, the South had undergone two years of drought, causing the crops to fail. The weevils multiplied and attacked the few remaining plants. The master, now under serious financial constraints, struggled to make austere provision for his slaves.

Soma read about when Moses was sent to free the slaves and how Pharaoh told his overseers not to provide straw for the bricks nor cut the number required. Their stories seemed similar as they were expected to deliver a harvest when none was in the field.

The winds blew cold in Virginia that year. For the second winter in a row there was little wood to heat the sheds that the slaves called home. Unrest among the plantation owners and their slaves grew to a point of open rebellion as the conditions threatened and took lives. In December of 1860 the first of the southern states seceded from the Union and began to solidify control of their lands.

When her father took sick and later died, Soma was left with just two brothers from her original family of nine. When the master of the plantation died that same year, his wife, Lillian, was left to run the plantation with just the overseer and the small workforce that remained.

Out of her element, she gave the overseer full control and blinded herself to the misery he perpetrated upon the slaves. Just as it seemed that things could not get worse, her daughter, Claire, returned with her new husband and the expectation that she could take up where she had left off. Claire's husband, Lamont, was what her father called a "dandy." He was a man who was born to privilege and had no concept of work. He, like Claire, had been born into money and it mattered little to either when it vanished.

Lamont always dressed as though he was on his way to a country club or political event. He would prance his way across the barnyard in order to avoid the droppings from the animals. "Strutting like a bantam rooster" was how some folk described the walk of the young man. Soma often looked up from her labors to see him standing nearby openly staring at her while she worked. Although she felt uneasy about it, she told no one.

If Soma had the will to fight when he first grabbed her, she might have prevailed because she was young, strong and inches taller than Lamont. But she had lived all her life under subjugation and had never thought to question the right or wrong of orders given by her masters. By the time she became alarmed and enraged it had come too late to stop his advances. When she tried, he struck her again and again until her cries subsided and the cocoon of darkness took her to some faraway place. He had taken the one thing she owned as carelessly as he would have killed a chicken for his meal, simply because he wanted it. She lay bleeding and beaten between the red brick walls of the two sheds. Her cold dark flesh was exposed to the sting of the harsh December wind as she lay on the frozen ground.

It was her younger brother, Clarence, who found her and tried but was unable to drag her to shelter. When he returned with their older brother the two of them were able to move her indoors. That was the last time she saw Clarence alive. He had taken his father's tobacco knife and gone to the big house to kill Lamont and had been shot dead on the front steps.

Two nights later, when the moon's glow was covered by heavy clouds, Soma and her brother, Steven, ran away from the only home either had ever known. Unknown to her, she carried a white man's child in her young womb.

Slavery was not an issue easily decided by man, not even an issue clearly defined by Scripture. Slavery and servitude are prevalent throughout the Old Testament and only slightly less common in the New. Guidelines abound that tell us how to treat and value our brothers and sisters regardless of their station in life. Everyone, it seems, is a slave to something, even in modern society. If not debt then drugs, the desire to succeed, or to be famous grips our hearts. If we are not literal slaves, we make ourselves slaves to the world around us by the choices we make. If not God, our master becomes something less, more worldly, less loving and caring ... sin.

Extraordinary

Depending upon what one uses as the benchmark, nearly anything could be termed as either ordinary or extraordinary. That which is exceptional will often, over the course of time, begin to be considered commonplace.

Taller than many, shorter than some, smarter than most but still less than a genius, Dan Brown enjoyed the benefits of youth and the privileges of being born in America. Having both parents living together in the same house made him the exception to the rule in modern American culture. Sadly his peers often had two or more pairs of parents involved to some degree in their young lives. Dan sometimes found conversations hard to follow and had on more than one occasion stopped and asked them to clear up his confusion regarding parents, stepparents, brothers and sisters, steps and halves.

The Browns were by all indications a very ordinary and normal family. Their demographics defined them as median in every respect, except for their love of the Lord Jesus. When a friend or member of their extended family questioned their commitment, Dan's mother would just laugh and say, "Not fanatical, just faithful." Betty knew from personal experience that to those not having eyes to see or ears to hear the calling of God's Holy Spirit, any explanation she could have given would not have been understood.

Jim Brown, on the other hand, was more vocal and outspoken than his wife, possibly because he knew how far his faith had brought him. As a young man he had "danced with the devil" on more than a few occasions and by God's grace had lived to tell about it. And tell about it he would, often tearing up as he relived a life that had included both drugs and alcohol. His witness was all the more effective because of his willingness to humble himself and share his journey. Seldom was his audience personally left untouched by his honesty.

Dan had a younger sister, Tina, or Christina Marie as she was called when she was in trouble. Tina had been just seven when her errant bicycle left the sidewalk and wandered into the street in front of their home. Although the passing car was moving slowly, the impact cost her hours in surgery and ultimately the loss of her spleen and one kidney. The event made a profound change in the family both spiritually and physically. In the hours when her life hung in the balance, Jesus became both very real and personal to each of them. Following her recovery each one chose Jesus as their Savior and was baptized as a statement of their faith.

Six years later the family faced another crisis that threatened to test their faith once again. It began with what the doctor had termed urethritis, a simple infection that had caused Tina a great deal of pain and suffering. The drugs had ultimately proven ineffective, and the infection moved into her kidney which began to shut down. The situation became critical and life threatening almost overnight with dialysis serving as the short-term option.

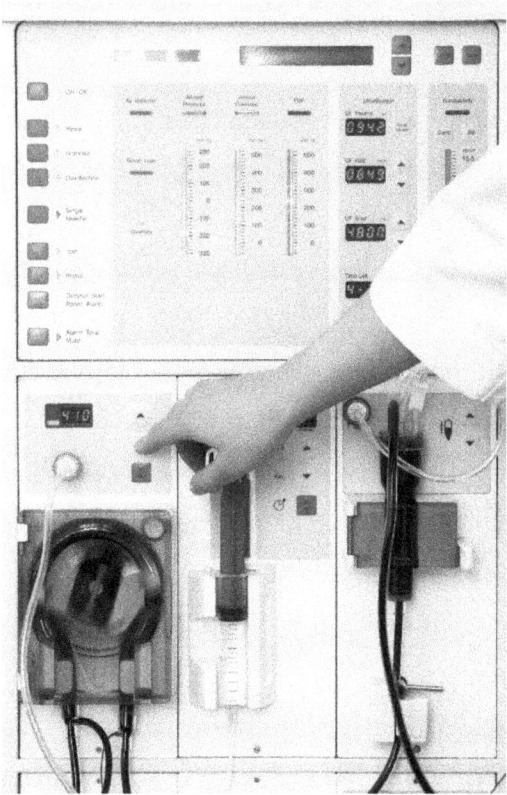

Dan had proven to be an exceptional athlete on the maple court and found his stride in his junior year. During his senior year the school was expected to repeat as state champions with him as their point guard and three-point wizard. Several colleges actively scouted him and invited him to consider accepting a scholarship. Life looked promising with a bright future and good education just within reach, until Tina's illness.

"It is critical that we make a decision as soon as possible," the doctor told them as they gathered in the hallway just outside of Tina's room. "It is possible the infection can be stopped and that her kidney will resume functioning on its own," he added. "But each day that passes makes it less and less likely."

"So what are our options?" Jim asked. "How long can she survive on dialysis?"

"Months, even years possibly," the doctor said. "But her quality of life as a young woman will be very poor, and there are some serious risks associated with it as well."

"Can I give her one of mine?" Betty asked, choking back the lump in her throat.

"Possibly," the doctor answered. "We usually like to start with family before we go to the national registry. The odds of a compatible tissue match are usually better with family."

"Let's get on with it then," Jim and Dan said almost simultaneously. "Test us."

Two weeks later, a second and similar meeting in the doctor's office included Tina as well.

"Jim," the doctor said shaking his head, "have you been in Africa or in the tropics?" Not waiting for an answer he continued, "You have tested positive for malaria. Have you ever been treated for it?"

Jim nodded, "I went on a mission trip a couple of years ago to Rwanda but came home feeling fine."

"Sometimes the carrier doesn't manifest symptoms right away and sometimes never," the doctor answered. "But either way you are not a good candidate. And Betty, your history shows breast cancer."

"But they said I was cured."

"And it is likely that you are," the doctor said smiling. "But it is also possible that you are still just in remission. You certainly wouldn't want to chance giving it to Tina."

"What about me?" Dan asked. "I don't have anything wrong with me."

"No, no you don't," the doctor agreed. "And you are a six-point match," he added. "The likelihood of a successful transplant is good."

Dan beamed, gave his sister a hug, waived his fist in the air and said, "Yeah!"

A look of pain came into the doctor's features. "I want to be up front with you. There are some downsides. Beyond the obvious dangers associated with any major surgery, it will change your life. You will have only one functioning kidney. In the event of disease or injury won't have a backup. You won't be eligible for military service, and you could be limited in your physical activities."

Dan was not dissuaded. "I don't care about all of that. She needs it, let's do it," he said with conviction.

The doctor nodded then added, "Just one last thing. It is unlikely that you will be allowed to play high school or college sports even after you have healed. Most will not accept the additional risk of injury that comes with a player having only one functional kidney."

Dan looked crestfallen, but for only a moment before regaining his smile and saying, "God gives us gifts so we may share them with others. Why else would we have two kidneys if we can get by with only one?"

Triumph

The sound of the bell sent the circle of spectators running toward the schoolhouse leaving Jake lying on the grass by himself. Bart hesitated, glowering over him, before spitting out a sentence laced with venom, and running off to join them. Only little Teresa remained, tears in her blue eyes, offering aid by extending her tiny hand.

"Are you all right?" she asked in her still small voice."

"Oh, I'm fine," Jake answered attempting to swallow his own urge to cry. "As fine as frog's hair."

"Your shirt is torn and your lip is bleeding," she said with a voice full of concern.

"Just the pocket," Jake said surveying his clothing. "Mom can fix it, good as new." He ran the back of his hand across his split lip and surveyed the blood and said, "Don't hurt me none."

But of course it did hurt. His lip, his pride, and his whole skinny 10-year-old frame ached. He was bruised but not beaten. He had not said "uncle" and given up. He had not let the bully get the satisfaction of feeling his fear or seeing him cry. He had defended Teresa. When he challenged Bart he had seen the hope in the eyes of the other children. At the start he had gotten in a few good licks before the older, larger boy pinned him to the ground.

Bart had been held back two years in school and like his three brothers used his age and size to intimidate and dominate. "Ruffians," he had heard them called by some of the women at church. Bart, no doubt, had learned to fight at home just to hold his own with his brothers and then found the younger smaller children at school an easy prey.

Two years his senior, nearly a head taller, and twenty pounds heavier than Jake, Bart lacked the skills to make full use of the advantage. Jake was fast and strong and didn't lose his temper easily. He'd have to remember to stay on his feet and keep out of Bart's reach if he had to face him again.

They walked toward the small, white schoolhouse together, straightening their clothes.

"Thank you," Teresa said softly, raising her eyes to his, a slight smile on her lips.

"Anytime," Jake answered, returning her smile then grimacing as his lip began to throb and bleed.

That is how it began in the fall of 1939 at a little, rural town in central Oregon. A newcomer to the area, Jake Billings had moved with his mother, father, and two sisters to a mining and timber community near John Day. Jake's father had taken a job as the superintendent of the local sawmill.

Jake was the youngest of the three children. His oldest sister was engaged and attended junior college. Nell, three years his senior, was just beginning the eighth grade at the same school as he. It was Nell who was eager to recount the story to the family over dinner that evening. Jake could see pride in her eyes when she told of how he had stood up to the bully who had tormented little Teresa and pulled on her pigtails.

Their father attempted to look stern when he said, "No one wins a fight."

But Jake could see pride in his eyes as well.

"I can fix the pocket, but I doubt I can get all the blood out of the shirt," Jake's mother said.

Jake knew they had little money to waste on replacing a perfectly good school shirt. Most of their income went to help pay bills and keep Helen in college. Nell worked part time at the local F.W. Woolworth store after school and on Saturdays, which gave her some discretionary income.

"His birthday's in a month," Nell said happily. "I just might have enough saved by then to buy my little brother a new shirt for his birthday."

Teresa was eight and an only child. She and her parents lived down the road from Jake's family. Her father ran a small dairy and delivered milk to the local community. Her mother was sickly and was seldom seen out of doors. When Jake and Nell walked by her house each day, she would run out, her red pigtails bobbing, and join them on their walk to school. Fair skinned like her mother, with big blue eyes and a multitude of freckles, she was a contradiction of personalities: shy and withdrawn around strangers, but outgoing and fun loving among her friends.

Jake had supposed that it was because she was quiet, smart, and well behaved that she seemed to be favored by the teacher and why Bart had made her the target of his scorn.

The summer Jake turned twelve he put on a growth spurt that gave him the appearance of a scarecrow. His father nicknamed him "Ichabod" after the character from one of their favorite books, *The Legend of Sleepy Hollow*. Teresa shortened it to "Ichi" and pronounced it with a lisp. Meanwhile, Helen married a serviceman from Seattle and moved west to be with him. Nell had just begun high school.

Teresa had not yet turned twelve when her mother died leaving her father alone, bitter, and ill equipped to raise a young daughter. Often the Billings family would invite them to church or over for a meal, but Teresa's father always deferred and sought solace in a bottle. Many nights Jake would hear a soft knock on the door and find Teresa there in her nightclothes waiting to be welcomed in and shown to Helen's room for the night. Nothing was ever said. No questions were asked when they sat down to breakfast with an extra chair at the table.

More often now the complaints of the cows with overfull udders would signal that John had not awakened from his drunken stupor. Jake's father would get Jake out of bed and send him across the pasture to relieve their distress before going off to school. When he turned 16, after a discussion with his parents, Jake went to John and offered to buy the business and give John a percentage. John happily agreed. He kept the farm, owned the livestock, and was responsible for their feed while Jake milked, bottled, and distributed it for 50 percent of the profit. While John's income went mostly to buy liquor and cattle feed, Jake's was split evenly between the family and a small but growing savings account.

Teresa lived with them nearly full time and helped around the house. She went home only to take food to her father. He seemed not to notice her absence.

By the time he turned twenty, Jake had added four more inches and 40 pounds to his frame and stood eye to eye with his father at five feet two inches. During the summer months he worked with his father, and was still running the dairy operation before and after the day at the mill. His sister Nell had married a druggist, lived in town, and was expecting a child.

In the fall of that year John became seriously ill, was diagnosed with advanced cirrhosis of the liver and required nursing care. Teresa moved home to care for her father. Jake was forced to cut his hours at the mill and take over the additional day-to-day operations of the dairy. In spite of their efforts John had little desire to live and the disease passed the point of recovery. On September 23, 1949, he was buried next to his wife. As the sole heir the court granted Teresa the conditional ownership of the farm and its assets, with oversight by a court-appointed guardian until she turned eighteen.

The small dairies sold whole milk to the dairy co-op who processed and bottled it for a fee and then allowed the independents to pickup and deliver the bottled milk to their customers. In later years they went into competition with the small dairies and would only buy the milk, but would not bottle it for resale. Because of the cost of setting up a bottling plant with only a few customers each, the dairy farmer became the victim of the monopoly that set and regulated prices to the consumer.

A senior in high school, alone in the world, and suffering the loss of both parents, Teresa went looking for something to comfort her pain. She had seen what alcohol had done to her father so she turned to her second family, the Billings. They in turn pointed her to God. The small community church in town was shepherded by a jovial Southern Baptist gentleman who had moved west and decided to stay. Bill Moore and his wife, Judy, had never been blessed with children, but like God, looked at each of their charges as their own. Teresa was no exception. They had known her since she was a small child and thought her to be one of Jake's sisters, since she always came and went with the family.

To their joy, Teresa embraced Jesus as her personal savior just a month later. She was baptized before the congregation just before Thanksgiving. As she came up out of the water Jake saw her as a strong, beautiful, young woman, not as the little sister that he had always loved and protected. He was conflicted, uncertain, and felt he had no one with whom he could discuss his strange new feelings. When he received his draft notice there seemed little to do but serve his country and put his personal life on hold.

~ ~

The North Koreans, whose communist ideology varied from their southern counterparts, had made their move against the south. When they attacked in June 1950 their intention was to put all of Korea under communist control. Jake had just turned twenty-one when his orders came and he boarded the train for boot camp at Fort Lewis, Washington. By the time his battalion reached the shores of Korea a bitter, cold winter had begun, leaving disconsolate men in a strange and inhospitable land fighting for and against men who looked markedly the same. It was the first time Americans were challenged to know if the man who stood next to them was friend or foe. Confusing and disheartening was how he described the war to his family.

He went from private first class to corporal and then to buck sergeant as men with integrity and leadership qualities rose to the surface when death and capture thinned the ranks. He led a squad of eight men, most of whom were facing their first conflict. Jake spent much of his time learning from the more experienced veterans, some who had seen action at the end of World War II. He soon gained the respect of his own men and his superiors.

Their forces, under joint United Nations Command, were over matched and found that the overwhelming numbers and knowledge of the terrain gave their enemies a tactical advantage. They moved ahead only to be pushed back later or be forced to stand and die defending some worthless piece of real estate. A hill with only a number or descriptive name like Pork Chop Hill, Heartbreak Ridge, or Naktong Bulge became the graveyard of many young men.

Jake's injury came not from battle but from the harsh climate when two fingers on his left hand became frost bitten and had to be removed. He spent only six days off the front lines before rejoining his unit with a new mitten over his left hand. At home the newsreels told of the victories and heroism of the American fighting men. In Korea the soldiers often had no idea if they were winning or losing in the conflict. As the long winter ended and became spring, the frozen ground was replaced by rain and mud slowing the movement of men and equipment.

Mail service was both slow and undependable. Letters came in bundles. They had clearly been sent over a period of weeks and sometimes months. When Teresa wrote, Jake always held his breath in fear of hearing she had wed. He resolved not to tell her how he felt, knowing it could only cause her additional pain and concern. He was also afraid that she may not feel as he did. When word of his father's heart attack came and he was forced to reduce his workload, Jake longed to return home to help. Teresa had sold off the dairy herd and leased the land to its new owner, but kept the farmland and the house. With the money from the lease and a part-time job in town she was getting by financially and keeping busy. Nell had given birth to twin boys, both healthy and vigorous.

As 1951 ended and ushered in 1952 it seemed the war had settled into a routine of move forward and retreat backward. Hold the high ground at all costs, then relinquish or die as you were overrun by the enemy. Two and a half years into the conflict with no end in sight, America's brave men were taken home in boxes or broken in body and spirit, and replaced by others full of enthusiasm and high hopes. Jake held the lifeless body of Jim, his closest friend, in his arms sobbing and questioning God's purposes. Tears came until there were no more, only to be replaced by a feeling of emptiness. For the first time since the fifth grade, when he had accepted Jesus, Jake began to question his faith.

Word came that Helen's husband had been badly wounded and sent home confined to a wheelchair and that Jake's father had been offered and accepted retirement. Nothing came from Teresa, Nell or his mother. When Jake received a bronze star for heroism he felt unworthy and guilty rather than pleased, knowing that many had done much more and had not been recognized. At the same time he felt pride for his men who received a "unit citation for bravery" for holding a critical piece of ground against overwhelming odds. Their courageous stand had bought time for a withdrawal and prevented the loss of many American lives.

Jake was less than a year away from the quarter of a century mark when the countries finally agreed to cease hostilities on July 27, 1953. At that point more than two and a half million lives had been lost. No victory dance for either side; only an imaginary line across a broken and beaten land resulted from the three years of war. He wondered if he could ever enjoy life again without feeling guilt. He didn't know if he could ever let go of the memories that haunted his nights.

Friends and family greeted the train at the station welcoming home their sons who were returning from a place that most had only read about. Jake's mother seemed to have shrunken in size. Her hair once thick and dark had thinned and turned gray. His father had taken on the shuffle of an old man, his shoulders now stooped, and his eyes lacking the sparkle of youth. Helen was not present. She was probably still in Washington caring for her injured husband and their children. But Nell, with her husband and two sons, looked vigorous and happy to see him as he stepped to the platform. Jake's eyes searched the crowd for Teresa, but found her lacking among the throng pushing and shoving to greet their returning heroes.

"The VFW is having a big welcome home party at the grange hall this evening," Jake's mother said as they drove toward home. "We have planned a private celebration tomorrow at Nell's if you feel up to it."

Jake smiled and nodded. "That sounds nice," he said.

"You're looking good, Son," Jake's father added. "You've put on a few pounds. Looks good on you."

"How are you doing, Dad?" Jake asked. "Are you staying busy, enjoying retirement?"

The melancholy look and sad smile answered the question before he spoke. "Okay, I guess," he answered. "I miss the mill and the men, and I hate trying to stay busy doing nothing."

Jake's father had been a "go-getter" all of his life, enjoyed work, and loved living life to the hilt. Even when his body was at rest, his mind was already busy planning his next activity.

Jake's mother took the lead. "You know what the doctor said," she reminded him for the hundredth time. "You've got to take it easy and not overwork your heart."

Jake disliked the way his mother seemed to be treating his father like a child, almost scolding him, but he said nothing. Jake was shocked by what he saw as the car turned off the main road and down the short lane which led to the only home he had ever known. The house looked small, old and almost abandoned. It seemed to have taken on the mood of its occupants who seemed to be just waiting to die. There were no flowers in the yard and no garden. Even the fruit trees were not flourishing as they once had. Maybe it was not so much that their home had changed, but that he had changed and was looking at it through different eyes.

"I've got your room all ready," his mother declared triumphantly as they got out of the car.

It felt strange to be home, stranger still that it didn't feel like home any longer. Suddenly he wished that he could just be a kid again, coming home from high school, dependent upon his mother and father to make all the important decisions for him, the future still full of dreams and promise. He wanted to go to bed and wake up believing that the last three years had just been a bad dream.

"I didn't see Teresa at the station," he said trying to sound casual. "Is she still around?"

His mother and father exchanged glances before his father answered, "She spends a great deal of time in town now, and at the rehabilitation hospital. She has contracted a case of polio and lost the use of her legs."

Jake's heart nearly stopped. He could still picture her running and jumping, her pigtails flying in the wind, waiting for him to push her in the tree swing, or playing tag on the school grounds. But he couldn't picture her confined to a wheelchair. Tears rimmed his eyes, and it became hard for him to breathe. No words came from his lips in answer to the news.

Finally he asked, "How long, how long has she had it?"

"Nearly six months since she first started having problems, but it has only been a couple of months since they officially diagnosed the cause," his mother answered.

As Jake thought back he realized it was about that time her letters stopped coming. It must have been about the time when her own burdens overwhelmed her and she no longer had the strength to share in his.

"I want to see her," he blurted as though the timeliness of his visit would somehow change things.

Jake's father nodded, "We'll leave early and stop by there before we go to the grange," he said. "Maybe she'll go over with us."

Jake went to his room, his mind confused and overwhelmed by what he had just heard. He knew for the first time, admitted to himself for the first time, that he loved Teresa and wanted to marry her. *What would she say? Did she feel the same? Would her illness change things between them?* He felt hopeless, lost and out of control. He began to weep. Suddenly he was racked with grief and emotion, his body shaking and tears long repressed streaming down his cheeks. When the tears finally stopped he felt weak but cleansed. A melancholy sadness replaced his grief. All of the pain, fear, and emotion of the past three years drained away, leaving him empty but at peace.

"God," he prayed, "You have known Teresa and me from before the day we were born. You brought us together and to Jesus many years ago. You know our hearts and the plans you have for us. Help us to know your will and give us the strength to do it. Amen." When he finished praying he closed his eyes and lay across his bed.

"Son," his father said quietly, "it's time we should be going to town if you are up to it."

"Thanks Dad," he answered. "I must have dozed off. Be right there."

Reluctant Hero

A great man, a man of insight and conviction, were some of the terms used to describe the tall, dark-haired man standing before the assembled crowd. His craggy face and deep-set eyes were framed by overly large ears, giving him an odd if not comical appearance. Were it not for the honesty and conviction that his manner and words conveyed, many would not have taken this man seriously.

Tall and lean, almost to the point of looking undernourished, he was an imposing figure as he stood and humbly accepted the introduction of his peers.

"My friends and colleagues," he began, "we are facing trials too large to imagine and looking for answers to questions too complex to understand. As men, the circumstance we face overwhelms us, defeats us, and leaves us without hope and living in despair. Our allies have become our enemies. Our faith is shaken. We reel under the weight of spiritual attack."

The crowd listened, enwrapped. Not a word was exchanged between them as he continued to speak.

"Were it not for the presence of God and His promises, we could count ourselves as already defeated."

This was not the speech they had come to hear. These were not the words that they hoped would promise victory. They were the words of truth, honesty and conviction. He made no attempt to sugar coat or minimize the seriousness of the circumstance in which they found themselves.

"Our enemies are not those on the battlefields, not the men who live and die for their beliefs. Our true foe is the Enemy of God. Our foe is the Evil One who fosters the greed, selfishness, stubbornness, cruelty and pride that have followed us since our fall from grace. It is not a battle that we can win with swords or cannons or by grit and wile. It is a battle that must be won by God, in each heart."

He hesitated before continuing. The room remained silent. No muted words or comments were audible in the room.

His strong voice seemed to break for an instant as he implored them to join him. "Will you pray with me? May we join our hearts as we lift up our voices together to our God and our Savior asking for His forgiveness and a new direction?"

~ ~

Years before a man much like him had spoken similar words to a divided nation, a nation under siege by the same enemy. And before that, another and another. Conflicts seem to bring out the best and worst in men simply because of the choices they demand. The one that gets fed is the one that becomes strongest. The one that controls you is the one you have chosen to follow.

~ ~

"Where will it all end?" she asked her husband as they drove home from the gathering.

He smiled knowingly, and then said, "Where or when?"

"I guess we know the answer to both, don't we?" she responded. "But I was not referring to the final victory or when Jesus will return to earth and set up His kingdom at the end of time. I meant how far must it go? How long will He allow man to reject Him before He raises up a leader who will lead our nation back to Him?"

"When Jesus came they were looking for such a man, a Messiah who would come as a conqueror and lead them out of slavery. But of course they rejected Him because He was not at all what they wanted. They wanted to continue to sin and overcome their enemies with weapons of war and not weapons of peace," he said with sadness in his voice. "Even Jesus, the Son of God, could not lead hearts unwilling to follow.

She nodded in agreement, her face filled with love for the man God had brought into her life.

"The answer to your question then," he said, "is when each of us returns to God, when we choose to seek His kingdom and His righteousness in our daily lives. When we fall to our knees in repentance. When that is our motivating passion we won't be as concerned about our national leaders. Israel demanded a king like all the other nations. They rejected God and His chosen leader and they got what they deserved.

She tried to lighten the moment. "You missed your calling. You should have gone into ministry."

But he would not accept her attempt to dismiss the seriousness of the moment and said, "Are we not all ministers? Isn't our witness a testimony of our faith?"

"Stop it," she said. "Talk to me about something unimportant for a moment."

"Where do you want to eat?" he said with a wry smile.

"How many were there?" she asked, referring to the town hall meeting.

"Too few," he answered. "Too few."

"I'd guess over two hundred," she responded trying to encourage her husband.

"Maybe, but how many heard? How many really heard and will take it to heart?"

"Fishes and loaves," she said. "The number doesn't matter, does it? He is able to feed the many from the few."

Smiling he said, "At least you were listening, and you understand. Yes, there is always enough to accomplish God's purpose. Even one is enough if empowered by God."

"Do you remember the little conversation Abraham had with God?" she asked, changing the subject.

"Which one?"

"The one where they haggled over the number of faithful required to restrain God from destroying Sodom."

"Sure do. I always wondered where Abraham found the courage to keep pressing God until he got what he got what he wanted.

"Are you him? Could you be the one God has chosen to help change hearts and lead us?"

"I doubt it. It would take a lot more than I have to give to make much of a difference."

They were eating dinner when the conversation resumed.

"You sounded like Moses," she said to him.

"At the hall?" he asked trying to remember what he had said that would make her compare them.

"No," she answered, "when you talked about changing hearts and leading us back to God."

He laughed, nearly losing control of the food in his mouth. "You about choked me to death," he accused.

She smiled. "Don't you remember how Moses kept refusing the job, making excuses until finally God got angry with him?"

"This is different. God did not offer me the job, and I did not say no."

She raised her eyebrows questioningly, hesitated, then said, "He didn't? Are you so sure? Just because you did not hear His voice boom out from the clouds doesn't mean He hasn't planted the seed in your heart."

~ ~

"I've never held office," he said into the phone. "And besides I'm too old. I turned sixty-five last August."

The voice on the other end persisted, saying, "Well, just think about it, and then get back to me."

"Who was that?" she asked, entering the room as he turned his cell phone off.

"Clyde," he answered, sounding embarrassed. "He and some of his buddies want me to consider running for office."

"What did you tell him?"

"I told him I was too old."

"What did he say?"

"He said to think it over and get back to him," he laughed. "Like I'd even consider running for governor."

"Governor? They want you to run for governor?" his wife said breathlessly. "Wow, I'd be the first lady of the state."

"Ha ha," he said. "Put your credit cards away. I can already see you shopping for a new wardrobe."

"Which party?" she asked, warming up to the idea.

"Which party what?" he said, sounding annoyed.

"Which party would you run on?"

"I'm not running," he said with conviction. "I already told him that."

"But, if you did, which would you choose?"

"I usually vote conservative."

"Conservative is not a party. It's an ideology."

"This is stupid," he said. "I have no intention of running for any office, least of all for governor."

"But if you did, which party? Humor me."

"The Reformed Christian Conservative Party," he said with a sigh.

"Never heard of it."

"That's because I just made it up," he answered with a smile.

~ ~

"Fact finding committee, what's that?" he asked Clyde. "A waste of time and money. By the way, whose time and money are we talking about here? Donations from where? Who has made donations to the coffers of an unwilling candidate? Really? You are telling me that a one-time unrehearsed gathering of a couple hundred people has brought that kind of support? No, I really hadn't given it any thought at all. Yes, I will. Yes, I will call you back. I promise."

"Honey," he called, "are you busy?"

She joined him in the den and asked, "What's up?"

"That was Clyde. It appears there is interest from some of those who attended the speech last week in the form of donations."

"Donations for what?"

"Apparently to fund a committee to consider the feasibility of a run for office."

"What did you tell him?"

"I said I'd consider it and call him back after we had time to talk," he answered.

"Are you asking my opinion? Do you want to know what I think?"

He smiled and nodded. "Let me have it."

"I think that you should do what I have been doing for the past week. Pray and ask God for direction."

~ ~

"Clyde, we may have a problem right off the start with my candidacy."

"What kind of problem?"

"I'm not a party man. I'm not sure that I'd fit the mold of either of our two political parties or be willing to support their ideologies across the board."

Clyde laughed. "You're a maverick. That's what they like about you. You come across as your own man. That's refreshing to most of us who follow politics."

"But is it practical to consider running against the machine and the backing that those parties provide?" he asked candidly. "Think about Perot, a man with money and good ideas who ended up as a spoiler."

"Granted, I agree with you in theory," Clyde admitted. "But you are discounting the support that really counts, God's."

"Do the study. But promise me that your pollsters will be up front about my stand concerning God and His leading our state. I am not interested in the office if it means compromise."

~ ~

"Did you suggest the name of your new party?" she asked smiling.

"No," he admitted. "I thought I'd wait and break it to him a little later, if and when we move forward with this silly idea."

"I rented us a movie," she said with her eyes twinkling. "It's called *The Reluctant Hero*. Maybe we should get some popcorn and cozy up together on the sofa."

Improvise Part 1

The rhythm of his steps was somewhere between a fast walk and a jog, a pace that he could easily maintain for hours. He seemed unaffected by either the elevation or the angle of ascent as the path took him higher into the mist-covered mountains. A young buck stood motionless in the aspen trees, bending into the scramble of nature – ears up, alert, muscles bunched for flight should it become necessary. But it was not necessary, for if the buck had been the prey it would have already been downed. He had smelled its musky odor minutes before and had seen the vapor of its breath in the coolness of the early morning.

It pleased him to know that he held the power of life and death in his hands and had granted life. He felt magnanimous, benevolent and almost godlike. God had given man reign over the animals of the earth, but not without also giving a sense of responsibility for His creation. A chipmunk caught his eye as it rushed to find shelter in the roots of a fallen lodgepole pine.

A pair of spruce grouse meandered in the trail ahead, seemingly oblivious to his approach. Had hunger been a problem he could have easily taken them with a club or rock. Fool hens, man called them, were the provision of God for the lost and hungry. God had purposely made them easy prey to preserve the life of a species He held in higher esteem. When they finally flew it was only a meter away, still within easy reach of any predator. A woof, a sound like a rapidly deflating air mattress, gained his attention and moved his hand toward his weapon. Slightly uphill to his left, standing motionless with its nostrils flaring was a young brown bear. It seemed uncertain as to what it should do about the intruder it had first smelled and then heard. It had, no doubt, just come out of hibernation, hungry and eager to recover the fat lost during the long winter.

It seemed puzzled at the scent of man. The strange scent urged caution, and caution provided escape to the foe who moved swiftly by him.

He thanked God that it had not been necessary to engage the bear in conflict, not because he was frightened but because it was an unnecessary confrontation. The bear would find suitable prey and later learn a disdain for man, but for now their mutual respect led them in different directions. One thought found its way to the forefront as he continued his run, *made in the image of God*. He had read it many times, but questioned what it really meant. *What was the image of God?* he wondered.

He could clearly picture the God who came to earth as a Savior, but not the One who sent Him, the One he called Father. He couldn't imagine the One who spoke the universe into existence with a word. The first seemed small and meek, while the second too vast and powerful to fit anywhere into his experience. To picture them both as one and the same was even more challenging. The voice of the third was the one who had always guided him. Known to him, but unseen, He had spoken to him since childhood, constantly offering choices and giving direction.

The trees opened into a clearing as he crested the ridge that overlooked the valley. He paused to scan the panorama that the ridge presented. He was awed by its majesty. He searched the valley for dangers that might be hidden in the dark shadows. He mentally recorded seven elk in a wallow below and a doe with two fawns walking a trail across the ridge above them. Far above an eagle circled, buoyed by the thermals created by the morning sun. No sound or smell alerted him to danger as he returned to the trail.

Without making an effort to check his watch he judged it was now about ten o'clock. He knew that he had at least four or five more hours to the summit. He was running along the southwest exposure, where the winter snows had been replaced by purple lupines and buttercups struggling to come to life. *This is how it must have looked at creation,* he thought to himself, *new, fresh, and unspoiled.*

The soil was becoming rockier and the brush and smaller trees yielded to the large old growth timber. Mist still hung over the valley 300 meters below and a shimmer of reflected sunlight outlined a small lake to the east. His path was less defined, less traveled now as the brush seemed stunted and less vigorous. He slowed his pace unconsciously aware of potential injury from falling rocks or poor footing. The altimeter on his right wrist read 7,815 as he followed the trail around a bend traveling due south. Kilometers away the snow-covered pristine peaks of the Canadian Rockies thrust upward like something heaved up from yesterday's creation of the world.

Dall sheep walked and grazed among the rocks. They sampled the sparse grasses without concern. Their white coats blended in with the patches of remaining snow. He could only judge his own progress by that which lay behind and what he could see across the canyon. He had been on the move for three hours since he had tethered his horse and begun the ascent on foot. Time was becoming critical to his mission. An hour's delay could mean the difference between life and death.

Dave was only twenty-six but already knew the meaning of responsibility. Young and eager, with the God-given body of an Olympic athlete, he quickly accepted when the mission was offered. He began to feel the value of each breath diminish as he approached the 8,800-foot mark and slowed his pace to accommodate. He knew that from this point on altitude sickness could cripple or disable him. He finally stopped, donned a light but substantial jacket, Gor-Tex coveralls, and gloves before entering the snowfield ahead. Moving slowly now, he chose his path carefully, skirting drifts and slides, choosing instead the rocky ridges where wind had cleared or diminished the accumulated snow.

The wind was blowing from the north fifteen to twenty kilometers per hour by his estimate. The temperature had fallen to negative eight degrees Celsius, but the wind chill had doubled that since he had begun. Caution, bred by experience, regulated his movements as he neared the first summit and removed the electronic locator from his inside pocket. The device was designed to both give and receive signals and had been tuned to the wavelength of the transmitter of the crashed airplane. It also sent a signal to the ground crew far below. They eagerly watched as the blips on the screen grew nearer to each other. To those who knew little about the operational limitations of an aircraft, a helicopter may have seemed the more viable rescue vehicle. Dave knew that was not so. Their lift capacity is diminished by thin air. High winds at high altitudes often make them a last resort for rescue.

It was his hope, indeed his prayer, first that there were survivors, and second that he would be able to help them move to a suitable retrieval site. Reports showed that three men had left Calgary in a small, twin-engine plane bound for Vancouver. It was known that after they left Calgary they encountered a storm over the big mountains where they were either forced down or crash-landed. Brief radio contact attested to their initial survival, but it lasted a few moments and was lost.

Dave traveled light in an effort to get to the plane. He hoped it wasn't going to be too little too late. His fifteen-kilo pack included medical supplies, food, water, rope, a small tent, signaling flares, plastic tarps, blankets, and a few items of warm clothing. The summit was in the neighborhood of 12,500 feet. Dave hoped to find the plane near or below the 10,000-foot level with minimal winds and snow. Anything higher would make a successful rescue nearly impossible.

He waited until he had the plane in sight before signaling base camp again. The plane appeared to have flipped after hitting, leaving one wing buried in snow with the other standing up like the fin on a shark. It took nearly an hour from his first glimpse of the plane until he was able to reach it. As he approached, he prayed, "Have mercy. Let them be alive." He pounded his fist on the tail section three times. The signal was returned from inside of the plane.

The right door was facing down and was one meter below the drifted snow. The left one was nearly perpendicular, making it impossible to reach. As he worked his way forward toward the nose he could see that the windshield was shattered. The bloody corpse of the pilot partially filled the opening. His body was already cold and stiff. Dave worked to free him and finish pulling him out over the nose of the plane. The wind pummeled the plane rocking it violently as gusts caught the standing wing. Dave moved to the leeward side of the plane finding relief from the deep snow and fierce wind. He placed the body in the shallow snow under the raised fuselage of the plane where the wind had formed a natural cave.

"Help us!" came the cry from inside.

With significant effort Dave climbed over the nose and followed his pack in through the gaping window of the plane. He could see that the survivors had retreated toward the tail section and were huddled together in the darkness. Dave put on an elastic headband and illuminated the interior of the plane with its LED lamp. Both men started speaking at once in a frantic effort to tell their stories. Dave took out a bottle of water for each of them and helped the nearest one open it. The other man was unable to raise his arms to accept it. He opened a bottle and held it as the second man drank nearly the entire thing.

Turning to the first man, Dave took control of the situation. "My name is Dave," he said, "and I'm here to help you get off this mountain. Are you injured?"

"I'm Paul," the first man said. "I think I have a broken leg. I can move but I can't stand."

"And you?" Dave said to the second. "What can you tell me about your injuries?"

"Blair Jones," he said. "I cannot feel anything from my neck down. I think my back is broken."

Dave took the man's hands one at a time. "Can you squeeze?" He felt no pressure. "It is more likely your neck than back," Dave offered, "and better for us."

"How could that possibly be better?" Blair asked.

"I am no doctor. I brought a cervical collar to immobilize your neck but didn't have room for a back brace."

The man nodded and then said, "Where's the rest of your team?"

"I'm it for now," Dave said, trying to sound in control. "The rest of them will meet us down below a ways."

Paul was a big guy. Dave could tell that by the way he filled up the limited space. It would be no piece of cake moving or lifting him if it became necessary.

"Any allergies, heart condition," he asked. "Are you taking any meds?"

"No meds," Paul replied, "but I am allergic to aspirin."

Dave handed him a Tylenol 222. "This will dull the pain some but will not put you out." He removed an air splint from his pack and partially inflated it. "You hungry?" he asked while digging into the pack for nourishment.

Both men ate from his larder of canned meat and dried fruit.

"Paul, I'll get to you in a minute or two, and then you can help me with Blair. That okay?"

Paul nodded.

"Blair, are you cold?"

"Freezing."

Dave installed the collar on him, took out a blanket, wrapped him from the chin down, and covered him with a plastic tarp.

"Okay, Paul, let's take a look at that leg."

As the light revealed the limb, Dave could easily see the leg was broken as it lay at an angle from his body.

"I need to cut your jeans and get a look at the break."

Outside the wind continued to howl and rock the plane.

"Let's get you into a seat where you can sit back and extend your leg," Dave said, "but don't try to move it. Let me do that."

Dave helped the larger man into one of the two rear-facing jump seats that had been torn from the floor during the crash.

"Okay, good," he said. "Stretch out your good leg and let me lift the bad one for you."

Paul groaned as he tried to move and then screamed as Dave lifted the other leg.

"Sorry partner," Dave said, feeling badly about the need to cause him pain. "You a Christian?"

Paul looked at him blankly.

"Do you know Jesus as your Savior?" he asked while working the leg into place.

With his mind trying to interpret the question, Paul momentarily forgot about his leg.

He looked angry when he answered, "You some Bible thumper, are you?"

"Nope," Dave answered smiling, "just a guy who asked God to help me run five kilometers up this mountain to find you and then asked Him to help us get out alive."

Paul did not respond.

"Blair, are you still with us?"

"Yep, I'm still here," Blair said laughing. "I'm not going anywhere soon unless Jesus comes and raptures us."

Dave laughed. "Paul, are those 222s starting to help?"

Paul thought for a moment. "Yep, I think so."

"Good, cause I need you to hang in there with me while I get this splint on your leg before it swells anymore."

Paul gritted his teeth and said, "Go for it."

In the confined space Dave had difficulty holding the leg still and situating the splint properly.

"I can't do this alone, Paul. You are going to have to help me."

"What can I do? I can't even reach it."

Dave took a short length of cord and tied it off to a support in the plane, then snugly through the laces of Paul's shoe.

"Okay. When I say, 'I need you to pull back against the cord,' that will hold your leg straight while I work the splint around it." He tore off several lengths of duct tape and stuck them to the plane within easy reach. "Ready?"

"As I'll ever be," Paul answered.

With the jeans out of the way, Dave worked the splint underneath the leg and then said, "Now."

Paul leaned back against the restraint, biting his lip as he did. Dave hesitated only a moment then brought the device up and around the swollen leg. He then snugged down the four Velcro straps. Beads of sweat broke out on Paul's lip and forehead.

"Got it," Dave said, inflating the air cast. "How about a drink?" He held up another bottle of water.

Paul laughed and said, "What I really need is a real drink."

Dave took a wool blanket from a storage locker and wrapped it around the injured leg, binding it together with duct tape.

"How's that feel?" Dave asked his new friend.

"Better, thanks. It just throbs now, unless I move it."

"I have a Vicodin for you, which will help some. I'll have to wait to give it to you. For now I need you alert so you can help me get you guys out of the plane."

"Sorry about before," Paul said contritely. "I'd about had it with hearing about Jesus from Blair and the pilot before the plane crashed. It kind of blew me away when you took up right where they left off."

"Blair, still no pain?"

"Well I have a bad headache, if that's what you mean. I think I banged it pretty good when we went down."

When Dave looked at Blair's head he saw no blood, but did see a noticeable swelling on the top center.

"Better not give you aspirin," he said, as much to himself as to Blair. "If you are bleeding inside the skull, it would make things worse."

He handed him an Advil. "Maybe this will help."

The wind changed direction and was flushing snow right into the plane. Dave took another blue tarp and zip tied it into place. Within a few minutes the space started to warm slightly.

They all jumped when the plane's radio crackled to life. Dave guessed that the wind rocking the plane had re-established the broken circuit from the plane's battery. He grabbed the mic and spoke into it slowly and deliberately. Immediately the ground crew responded. As he explained their situation he also explained the futility of attempting a basket air rescue at their altitude. Winds were steady at thirty kilometers with gusts of forty to fifty at times. Visibility was three kilometers and decreasing. His watch showed that it was after three o'clock already.

"I need a medical opinion," Dave said.

"Dave, this is Bert. What's on your mind?"

"I've got a compound fracture secured without bleeding on 222s. No sign of shock, alert and complaining," he said, smiling at Paul.

"I am not!" Paul shot right back. "I just asked for a good, stiff drink."

"And," Dave continued, "a second with no feeling in arms or legs, large contusion on his skull midline with swelling, but no discoloration. I have him in a neck brace on Advil. Advise."

"The paralysis could already be permanent. Or it could be temporary due to swelling and pressure at the brainstem. You must find a way to immobilize the head and neck before transport. Keep him warm and hydrated. Check the pupils often for uneven size or discoloration. Are you able to ride it out until morning?"

"Seems like the only option. Pray for a clearing during the night and no wind in the morning."

"Already have," Bert said. "We've all been praying since you set out this morning."

Dave turned off the radio and one of the cabin lights to save the battery. "You heard it all men," Dave said, "our best chance will be to remain here tonight and start out bright and early in the morning."

The second seat had also loosened in the crash. When Dave pulled it up beside Blair, the extra weight on that side caused the plane to lean. The plane settled at a forty-five degree angle. Dave adjusted the seating for the men, trying to keep their heads vertical as the new position changed their perception of up and down. The plane seemed to be moving with the wind and settling into the void where he had placed the pilot's body. At first it horrified Dave that the plane might settle right on the body, but then he reasoned that such an event would save it from predators and preserve it for later removal. The wind seemed to have increased outside, but the confines of their space were comfortable as mounting snow along the fuselage provided insulation. Dave gave each man more food and water. He gave Paul a Vicodin and suggested they try and get some rest.

It was only seven o'clock when he turned out the small cabin light after utilizing whatever he could find to insulate the men from the cold. Paul was lying in one seat, with his head slightly elevated, both legs outstretched and well covered. Blair was lying nearly flat. He was wrapped up like a mummy in blankets and plastic. Dave settled in on some of the loose baggage and covered himself with the final tarp.

Sometime during the night, in the blackness of their manmade cave, their world turned upside down, literally. Dave was awakened with a feeling of movement followed by screams. The fuselage moved and settled into the snow just as though it had landed properly. That of course was a mixed blessing. Although it provided an exit through the side door, it caused the injured men both fear and pain as their beds tumbled into each other. Dave attempted to turn on the cabin light only to find it had been disabled by the movement. He finally used his own headlamp to illuminate and assess their new situation. Blair was pinned against the hull with Paul on top of him. Paul was struggling desperately to move himself off of his friend. Dave's light calmed them. He helped Paul to rise and placed the seat underneath him before lowering him back into it. Together they rolled Blair's seat upright with him still anchored to it. Dave had done a good job of strapping him to the horizontal seat. He was frightened but not injured further. The wind had undercut whatever snow had been supporting the plane in its former position, allowing the plane to settle into its current one.

A glance at his watch showed that it was a little after three o'clock. The temperature had dropped considerably causing the frightened men new discomfort. Dave lit two survival candles and shut off his headlamp. The glow of the candles seemed to give warmth to their surroundings well before it began it chase away the chill of the morning. Snow caves are well heated by a single candle. A single candle glowing in the darkness provides the warmth needed to endure and the promise of rescue and survival. No one seemed eager or able to get back to sleep, so they shared a snack and more water and began to talk about how they could get down the mountain. Dave's plan was to ferry them down individually using the blankets and plastic tarps to protect them from the harsh weather. He did not talk about how he planned to keep Blair immobile, because he was not yet sure how he could make that happen.

As they visited, the temperature increased a few degrees.

Paul turned to Dave and asked, "Just what is the point of all this talk about Jesus dying for my sins? Who are you guys to be talking down to me about sin?"

Dave thought for a moment then said, "Do you believe that God exists, that He alone created the world and all that is in it?"

"Yes. I don't question the existence of God, never have."

"And you do know the story of the Garden of Eden and Adam and Eve?"

"Yeah sure, everyone knows how the snake conned them into eating the forbidden fruit."

"Good. Let's begin there. And another thing. You are being forced to trust me with your life up here on the mountain. I am going to ask you to trust me with your eternal life as well. You're going to have to trust me on both counts."

"You're pretty blunt." Paul said, smiling.

"Listen carefully to me. Where we are right now is about as safe as it gets. When we start out in the morning there's a real possibility that we may not make it."

"That's comforting to know," Paul said with a slight laugh.

"What I'm saying is that life is uncertain. Your pilot and Blair both knew that when they started talking to you about salvation yesterday. Now he's gone and there's nothing we can do to change where he spends eternity. The decision he made while he was alive determined if he is with Jesus in heaven or in the eternal darkness of hell."

Both men were listening carefully now.

"If I get injured and cannot pull you men out, we'll probably all die of exposure before we are found. We could get lost, get swallowed up in an avalanche, or go off a cliff. It is and has always been in God's hands. Our only choice is to believe and trust in Him or not. God is eternal. He is perfect and without sin. He will not live in the company of sin."

"So what is sin?" Paul asked. "What are we talking about here, the Ten Commandments?"

Dave ignored his question and asked, "What do you do, Paul?"

Paul looked surprised but answered, "I'm a salesman."

"Do you own your own company?"

"No, but I'm its top salesman."

"Who makes the rules for the company?"

"My boss. He owns the place."

Dave nodded. "And you, Paul, do you always agree with your boss's rules?"

Paul smiled and answered, "Heck no! He makes a lot of decisions that make no sense to the salesmen."

Dave smiled. "So you complain a little, but you follow the rules just the same because he is the boss, right?"

Paul nodded.

"So back to your question, Paul. Sin is whatever the boss says it is, and God is the ultimate boss. The whole universe is His. He made it. He owns it. He loves it and wants it to work in harmony with Him. Whatever sin is, it displeases and offends God. He cannot allow it in His presence. Who would want an eternal home that welcomes the kind of garbage we have down here? When He created Adam and Eve they were perfect and without sin, just as He is. He actually walked and talked directly with them. But when they chose to disobey Him it made a separation between Adam, Eve, all their offspring and God. As I said earlier, God loves His creation and wants to have the original relationship back again. He could have just forced man to do things his way, but instead He gave us the freedom to choose for ourselves. He gave us the right to say no to Him, to not love Him as He loves us, and to reject an eternal life with Him. Paul, does your family do anything special for Christmas?"

"Of course," Paul said.

"What is it that you are celebrating? I assume that you give gifts to one another. It's amazing how we spend so much money and work so hard to make that holiday special without reflecting on the real purpose. When Jesus, God's only Son, came to earth as a baby, He came to accept the penalty of sin for us. He came to restore us to the relationship that He originally had with Adam and Eve." Dave stopped talking and looked at Paul. "Am I making any sense to you?"

Paul looked at Dave reflectively and said, "This was all so long ago. How could it all still apply to us today?"

Dave smiled. "God is eternal. So we, being made in His image, are eternal as well. The Bible tells us that even though we shall die, yet shall we live. This means that even though each of us will die once here on earth, all of us will live on as God does, forever. Our only decision is where to make our reservations."

Blair laughed. "That is the first time I have heard it put that way."

"What about Sam, the pilot? Where is he right now?" Paul asked.

Dave shook his head. "We have no way of knowing for certain, but after hearing what you said about his eagerness to witness to you, I'd bet he is walking with Jesus right now. Sam loved you because Jesus loves you, because God the Father loves you. That is why he was trying to make sure you reserve a spot for yourself by accepting Jesus as your Lord and Savior."

"Lord and Savior, what's that?"

"Lord is the term used to describe the one you recognize as your boss, the one who gives the orders. Savior is one who saves you by taking the bullet for you or paying the penalty for your mistakes. When we invite Jesus into our lives we choose to reject sin, ask forgiveness for both past and future sin, and accept that He has already died for us."

Paul looked grim. "So we really don't have a choice then do we? It's His way or hell."

Dave disliked how the truth felt cold and unloving to him, but knew that God's plan did not include grading on a curve.

"There can only be one in charge. Your boss knows that and you know that. God, our ultimate boss, doesn't lead by consensus of opinion. God loves us too much to blur the lines of right and wrong. He does not want to be separated again from any of those He loves. He is fair, just, loving and merciful. He waits for you to make your decision and wants it to be the right one, but He will not force you. Paul, do you suppose He chose to take Sam rather than you knowing that Sam had chosen wisely and that you still needed time to make your decision?"

"So Sam had to die because I did not take all this seriously enough?" Paul asked, with eyes rimmed with tears. "Did I cause him to die because I was stubborn?"

"No, Paul. God chose when the time was right to call Sam home. He might have used his passing to help you listen and maybe accept His offer of salvation. God doesn't want anyone to perish. God is concerned about us in the long run, while we are more short term in our thinking."

The candlelight reflected tears running down Paul's cheeks. His voice choked as he asked, "Will you show me how to do it? I don't want to wait until tomorrow when it may be too late. I want to make sure I have a chance to spend forever with my friends and family, and Jesus."

Dave and Blair closed their eyes and Paul followed suit.

"Father, forgive me for my sins," Dave said. "Thank you for sending Your Son to take my penalty for sin. Please live in my heart and help me to accept you as my Lord and Savior. Amen."

Paul repeated the prayer word for word.

Blair added, "And Father, if it is your will preserve and protect us as we leave this place of refuge and help us return safely to our families."

To be continued.

Improvise Part 2

Dave crawled from the plane's door into the waist-deep snow that had blown around the plane. Coiled in his pocket was a bone saw comprised of two steel rings connected by a lightweight braided cable that had been infused with carbide chips. The abrasive chips could easily cut through bone, wood, or light metal simply by drawing them back and forth across the surface.

The wind bit into his coat and small pieces of ice blasted at his exposed face as he attempted to cut off a section of the wing. He hoped it would serve as a snow sled gurney. He estimated that they would need it to be about two meters in length. He added another hand span for good measure. He began his cut just beyond a uniform line of blind rivets assuming they would be connected to a support under the aluminum skin. About one-third of the way across, he couldn't feel his fingers, so he returned to the cabin of the plane. Blair could not see out the window from his horizontal position, but Paul had watched the progress and reported it to him.

"So Dave, how's the weather, eh?" Paul said, with a grin.

"I think we are in for an early spring," Dave responded. "The sun is shining somewhere behind those clouds. I figure another month or so." He took off the gloves and warmed his fingers in opposite armpits.

"There's a baklava or two in my gear bag," Blair offered. "You're welcome to it."

As he rummaged through the man's bag he found a rubber coat, pants and a toque. "What's with the rain gear? What were you planning to do in Vancouver?"

"Fishing," came the reply from both men.

"We were going salmon fishing," Blair said.

"Thank you, Lord," Dave said quietly to himself. "Did you both bring rain gear?"

"Sorry," Paul replied, "I was going to buy mine when we got there."

"I'm going to borrow your rain gear, Blair. Is that is all right with you?"

He gave each man the remainder of the dried fruit and one of the last three bottles of water to share as he slipped away from the plane once again. This time, however, the rain suit prevented the wind from penetrating and the toque diminished its sting on his face. Dave stopped twice to warm his hands but did not find it necessary to return to the plane until the wing tip dropped free. Dave judged the section at just over two meters long and a shade over one and a half at its widest spot. It was light, less than twenty kilograms he guessed, making it necessary to secure it from the wind.

Back inside the fuselage Dave visited with the men as he laid out his plans. "I doubt I will have the strength to take one of you all the way down and then return for the other," he admitted. "So the plan is for all of us to go out together using the wing as a toboggan. Once I get you out we'll have to hurry to get you on the wing and covered up. If we don't move quickly there will be a serious hypothermia threat. There's a sheltered place right under the wing where the wind is not as fierce. I'll get Paul out first and get him up where he can lean against the wing. He can then help me get you out, Blair. I've got to go back out and punch some holes and attach some zip ties through them to provide a way to strap you on."

"Sleeping bags! Sleeping bags!" Blair said excitedly. "Sam had us stow our sleeping bags in a rear compartment in the tail."

"That's right," Paul agreed. "I had forgotten we even brought them."

Dave felt a surge of encouragement and thanked God once again for His provision. "Thank God!" he said aloud. "I'll get the wing ready, return with the bags, and we'll get Blair into some warm, dry clothes. I'll put him into a bag before bringing him out.

His watch showed a quarter to eight. He gave Paul another Vicodin before moving outside to prep the wing. With a Leatherman multi tool he used the leather punch to make holes in the thin aluminum skin of the wing. He put them along its length in pairs before fishing the heavy-duty zip ties through each set of two. When he was finished he had twelve holes with six loops on each side. He returned inside the plane with one of the mummy bags. He then used his knife to cut all eight sets of seatbelts from their moorings on the floor. Outside once again, Dave installed six of the eight belts to the wing using the loops and additional ties to secure them. He wrapped each with duct tape to keep them from coming loose.

It just might work, he thought to himself. *Si Dieu le veut.*

Near the tip of the wing and again at the other end he found a substantial support where he cut access holes and attached lengths of rope with the intention of using one to pull and the other as a brake when going downhill. Back inside the plane he fashioned the final pair of seatbelts into a harness to go over his shoulders. Dave hoped it would help to keep the rope from biting in as he pulled the toboggan. The men shared another bottle of water and drank a thermos of cold coffee that had been found under the pilot's seat. They were down to four energy bars - two of which Dave reserved for himself, the other two as a mid-trail snack for his guests.

"The good news," Dave said, "is that the way home is mostly flat or downhill. The bad news is that it is mostly flat or downhill. So I'll be pretty much pulling all the time on the flat and trying to slow us down when we come to the steeper areas."

They each said a quiet prayer before preparing to leave. Dave hoped the Vicodin he had given Paul was kicking in by now, but not so much that he would be unable to help get Blair out of the plane.

"Paul, let me help you get to the door. Once I'm out you'll want to come out headfirst so I can catch you and lower you onto the wing and then down to the ground. I think your leg is protected well enough that you won't damage it any further. Once you are out and situated, I'll come back in for Blair and send him out to you the same way. Leave him on the wing until I can get out and lower him onto the toboggan."

"You make it sound easy," Paul laughed. "You do this often?"

Dave smiled at his new brother in Christ. "Just once, counting this time."

Blair was wrapped like a caterpillar in a cocoon with extra blankets around his torso and legs then draped in a plastic tarp and duct taped.

Dave crawled out with his own pack and then signaled for Paul to follow. When Paul came out he groaned as he put a little pressure on his broken leg. In spite of the obvious pain he kept moving until he was on the stubby little portion of the wing that remained attached to the plane. Dave swung Paul's body around perpendicular to the wing and began to help him get lowered to the ground. Paul had not said a word the entire time, but his face became pale as he touched down on the ground.

Dave grinned at him and said, "We Christians have a verse for this from the Bible: I can do all things through Christ who strengthens me."

Paul tried to smile back but failed.

"Get your bearings for a minute," Dave instructed. "Try and find a position where you can put your weight on the good leg and wedge yourself against the wing and the side of the plane."

Dave crawled back inside where Blair remained alert.

"How'd he do? Is he all right?"

"He did fine. How about you? Are you ready for a sleigh ride?"

Blair smiled. "Ready when you are. Try the radio."

Dave looked at him strangely. He then nodded and moved toward the cockpit. When he flipped the switch and keyed the mic the radio crackled to life. Dave gave a quick update to the base camp, well aware that Paul remained outside in a tenuous position. He then slid both Blair and his seat out the door and onto the stub of the wing. Paul did what he could to help from the other side. Dave thanked God that Blair was a small man, nearly forty-five kilos lighter than Paul even with the weight of the seat. When Dave got to the ground Paul was holding his friend's head in his hands, looking right into his eyes, and talking softly to him. He could not hear what was being said, but understood that the big man was coaching him up, preparing him for the trip.

"Paul, you go first. Let's get you comfortable in the bag and out onto our makeshift toboggan."

Paul smiled. "Comfortable, eh? This is a heck of a place to be worrying about my comfort."

Dave had placed the wing on a snowdrift about one meter tall, making it just the right height for Paul to sit down. Dave unzipped the bag and installed it on him like a giant tube sock.

Dave began to laugh. "You look like a huge sausage."

All three men laughed as Dave strained to pull the man onto the wing and wrap him in the blue tarp. Next, Dave eased Blair, still on the flattened jump seat, beside his friend and began the chore of securing both to the wing using the seatbelts.

Dave had worked up a sweat and feared a chill, but there was little he could do about it. What he feared even more was the threat of predators between here and the pickup point. Dave couldn't get rid of the thought of the scent of blood being carried by the wind. While the sleeping bags and blue tarps would provide some cover, Dave knew that the bear he had passed on the way up would easily pick up the scent. He could only hope that the bear had left the area. He also knew that wolves were known to exist in these mountains. He knew that the handgun he was carrying would probably not be sufficient to fend off an attack. He feared that they would be easy prey if the scent were to give them away. Dave tried to move the gun to a more accessible position without alerting either Blair or Paul.

Just then, Dave was reminded of a Scripture verse he had once known: *Whenever I am afraid, I will trust in You.*

He taped his rubber pants at the bottom and the sleeves at the wrists to keep out snow and retain body heat. He then donned his makeshift harness and moved to the front of the wing.

"Time for a little prayer," he told his companions. "Jesus bring us back safely or take us home to be with You."

As he began to pull he quickly discovered it moved along quite easily on top of the powdered snow. He leaned his body into the webbing of the seatbelt, which pulled both from his waist and shoulders.

"You both all right?"

Both men tried to respond through the drawstrings of their head covering but went unheard because of the sound of the wind. After a couple hundred meters, the ground began a gentle descent and Dave found the wing often bumping the back of his heels. As the slope steepened he reattached himself at the rear of the wing to slow its forward momentum. He quickly found that pulling was easier than trying to brake the several hundred-kilo burden as gravity beckoned it downward. He also learned that slow and easy was the wisest course of action. If it got out of control he knew he would be unable to stop it. Finally they came to a flat area where he took a much-needed breather.

The area was iced over and smooth. It looked like a Zamboni had been up here. He didn't know if that was going to be a good thing or not.

He unlaced the head coverings to allow their faces to be seen and then asked, "So have you enjoyed the trip so far? Is there anything I can get you?"

"I think I need a rest stop," Blair said, smiling. "Any chance we can pull over?"

Paul seemed to be out of it. The painkiller had done its work and the fatigue from the ordeal had done the rest. Dave gave Blair the last sip of their water and a bite of an energy bar. After starting out again, he quickly found that following a trail was not an option. The trails were side hilled while the wing wanted to go vertical and straight toward the bottom. Scouting ahead became a necessary diversion, further slowing their progress and tiring Dave. He would walk ahead to choose the best route between rocks, trees, cliffs and elevation extremes before returning and assuming his burden.

When he keyed his transmitter, he received no answer from the base camp. Finally they came down a ridge that offered an extreme vertical option on three sides without any chance of return. Dave was forced to use his rope and available trees to slow the descent of the wing. At noon Dave was fatigued and questioned his ability to continue. He estimated that they were still two kilometers away from the pickup point. The elevation was 8,421 feet when he stopped to check on the men. Blair appeared to be well but tired, and Paul was still asleep. Several handfuls of snow wet his lips but provided little in the way of the hydration that he so badly needed. They were still well above the snowline, which offered little chance of fresh water and no time to find it.

Finally after another hour they came down a gradual ridge to an open knob that gave Dave a clear field of vision. In the distance he saw the sparkling gem of a lake he had seen on the way up. Somehow it gave him reassurance and strength.

This time when he keyed the transmitter the camp answered. "Dave, this is Bert. How are you doing? How are the men?"

"They seem to be riding well," Dave answered. "Can you tell by my beacon how far I am from the pickup point?"

"Hard to tell distance," he answered, "but you are still nearly 500 meters too high. The pickup is right where the snow gets patchy. It's a bald clearing south and east of your position. How are the winds?"

"Depends," Dave replied. "It's calm where I am now and ten to fifteen when I'm in the open. No falling snow."

"Good. I'm going to ask the boss to make a run up to the pickup site and drop me off. I'll come up and give you a hand. How does that sound?"

"Like an answered prayer. I'm dehydrated and starting to cramp up. If I could get my hands on some water I'd be a new man."

"Rest up Dave. I'll see you in about half an hour."

Dave looked up at the clearing sky. Blue was beginning to show between the clouds. He closed his eyes and said, "Thank you Lord."

His focus was brought back to earth when Blair called out. "How are we doing out there Dave?"

Dave walked to the wing and loosened the bunting, allowing him to see Blair's face. He smiled. "We are doing fine now, Blair. How about you?"

"Snug as a bug. No pain. Just tired and eager to get home."

"We've got help coming up by chopper and then on foot to give us a hand to the extraction point. He should be here soon. Hang in there."

Dave unlaced the strings of Paul's hood. Paul's eyes opened with a dreamy look in them, and he said, "Are we there yet?"

Dave laughed. "Nearly. We should be at the pickup point in an hour or so. How's the leg?"

Paul thought for a minute before answering. "It must be fine. I can move my toes and it doesn't hurt."

Dave gave him a bite of energy bar and said, "Sorry, I don't have anything to wash it down with. We are out of water but have more on the way."

"Fine with me. I've got a full bladder already and don't want to rock the boat."

Fifteen minutes had passed when Dave first heard the sound of the chopper coming up the mountain and five more when he had a visual. It still seemed distant when it settled out of sight into the tree line below. As he lifted his eyes from where the chopper disappeared from view, Dave thought he saw movement in the trees. He couldn't quite make out what it was. Once again an intense fear came over him. He had never felt so helpless. How could God fail him now when he was so close and had come so far? Dave reminded himself of a truth that had seen him through so many tough spots: *Trust in Him at all times, you people; Pour out your heart before Him; God is a refuge for us.* He was reaching for his handgun when his locator beeped signaling a call. The sound shot through him like a bolt of electricity.

"Dave, this is Bert," came the welcome voice. "We've landed safely. I should be there in a few."

"Get up here in a hurry," Dave said, after he had composed himself. "We may have wolves in the area. I could sure use your help. Make sure I know that it's you coming. Wear an orange vest or something."

"Ten-four. I'm on my way, and I'll bring the rifle."

"That was Bert, a friend who is on his way up to give us a hand. The chopper has landed about a click and a half below us and is waiting for our arrival." Dave searched the horizon for more signs of movement. His body was damp with sweat from all his exertion, which only compounded the chill he felt. He would rather be moving than standing guard, but he knew he couldn't defend them very well if he was wrapped in the harness. He found it hard to judge the air temperature but could still see his breath when he exhaled. After about fifteen minutes, which felt more like an eternity, Dave saw Bert making his way through the trees. Safe at last, he breathed a huge sigh of relief.

As Dave reflected on the last twenty-four hours he was amazed at how much life God could pack into a short time frame. He reveled at how each need had been provided for at just the right time. Where had the idea to use the wing come from? It seemed like the right equipment to utilize. The minimal food and water proved to be just enough. Of course he knew the answers and thanked God mentally for His provision. He thanked Him also for the circumstance that had led Paul to faith and felt privileged to play a part. He was still immersed in thought when he heard Bert's voice.

The men were thankful for the food and water Bert brought with him. Soon Dave filled his friend in on both the strengths and weaknesses of their improvised transport vehicle.

"If we try to side hill, it will beat us to death and could possibly even cause the wing to flip. I found that out the hard way at the first downhill when I tried to stay on my original trail."

Bert understood and agreed.

"Are there any flat areas or hills between us and the chopper?" Dave asked his friend.

"A couple of level spots, and a couple of rocky verticals we will need to skirt around. There are some thick stands of trees, but mostly open ground if we stay on the ridge."

As they began, Dave took the lead rope, mostly giving direction to the front end while Bert slowed it from behind. As the terrain became steeper Bert struggled to keep the speed under control forcing Dave to join him at the rear until they neared a thick stand of fir trees. They had traversed several hundred meters before God gave them rest in the form of a level barren knob. Leaving Dave with the rifle and the injured men, Bert walked ahead scouting out the area. He found that the flat ended abruptly at a rock cliff that dropped ten meters before resuming the snow-covered descent. To deal with it they attached every scrap of rope they could find to the rear of the wing. As it got to the cliff, Dave guided it to the side while Bert stood at the top as an anchor to slow its decline. Just as the line came to its end Dave pulled the front hard to the side causing it to swing back toward the ridgeline. They joined their two new friends at the wing and rested for nearly half an hour before continuing.

The next challenge came in the form of a stand of trees that extended completely across the ridge. There was no way that the wing could be wedged through this barrier. The men were forced to use the bone saw to fall several of the smaller trees. This made it possible for them to wind their way between the larger ones and finally out beyond them. This significantly delayed their progress and left both men completely exhausted. As the snow-covered mountainside became steep, they were forced to belay the rear rope around available trees to slow the wing's downward movement.

While they rested again on a level spot, the locator crackled to life. A voice from the pickup site greeted them and asked about their progress. "We show you about 100 meters above our location. You should have a visual on us after you clear the next rise."

Both Dave and Bert felt invigorated by the welcome news, which they repeated to Paul and Blair.

When they finally reached the pickup point Blair was loaded onto a backboard and Paul onto a stretcher. The chopper took them directly to the Calgary hospital. Both men were admitted, x-rayed, and treated for their injuries.

A second chopper picked up Dave and Bert and flew them into Canmore where they got a chance to rest and get something to eat. The search and rescue team retrieved Dave's pickup, horse and trailer, and returned them to him in Canmore. The next day Dave and Bert drove to the Calgary hospital to check in on them and get more information for their official reports. Blair had regained some response in his hands and fingers indicating there was no serious spinal cord damage. Swelling along the spinal cord had caused the temporary paralysis. Paul's leg hung in a trapeze suspended over his bed. He would be in a cast for some time before he could begin physical therapy.

As they said their goodbyes and started to leave, Dave turned to the men and said, "Maybe we'll meet again under better circumstances."

Paul smiled and answered, "That is guaranteed my friend. Jesus made it certain for me."

Fantasies of the Flesh

If there is any place where you should feel safe, it should be in your home. It doesn't seem right that you should have to worry for your safety in your own bedroom, and yet he did. The fear had begun early in his life, but he could not remember just when or why. As an infant often struggles to stay awake, and ultimately loses the battle to fatigue, he had the same challenge for as long as he could remember. He made up games in his mind to help stay awake, buried his head under the covers with a flashlight, but always, always sleep had come. With sleep came the haunting memories and the unbelievable creatures in his dreams – nightmares to be more precise.

As a young child he had attempted to describe to his parents the horror that lived in his room. They had never taken him seriously or believed his safety was in danger. That changed the night his sister disappeared. He had tried to tell them, warn them, but even then they continued to believe it had been an intruder who had kidnapped their baby. He supposed their disbelief gave them hope. It gave them something to cling to, with the possibility that somehow, someday she may be returned.

Had they known the truth, as he did, there would have been no hope, no chance of a joyous homecoming. He was only five when she'd been taken. He was seven now, old enough to know that it was not his imagination that lurked under the cover of darkness. For the most part they did not take a solid form, made no audible sound, and lived an existence outside of the laws ruling over the world that all could see. Yes, they had spoken to him many times, but more often the words were formed in his mind, torturing and frightening him beyond description. Once he had tried to talk about it to his best friend Tommy, but Tommy made fun of him in front of his classmates and called him a baby. He could still feel the shame and embarrassment of that moment. So he withdrew and stopped in his attempts to convince others of the peril that stalked him.

They seemed to take pleasure in his discomfort, in the paralyzing fear that they brought to his heart. Over the years some had become familiar to him. Their forms were predictably disgusting. Others, however, seemed to be visitors, who came infrequently and changed in both form and purpose. Sean was familiar with Transformers, the current rage among his peers. These fictional characters were alien mechanical devices that could assume and reassume forms and shapes. However, they were created from man's imagination and were both good and evil, with the good always able to overcome the evil. In his experience there was no corresponding character representing good - only evil.

His parents had sought solace for little Molly's loss by pursuing religion. They tried to understand what purpose her disappearance may have served. At first they had searched for answers at the Catholic church. They also tried a Protestant church. They had not sought God on their own. They looked to men of the cloth as to the ways of God. In the end it had failed, for no man truly knows all of God's purposes. Sean, however, had met a young intern, a pastor in the making, who served the youth group at the Baptist church. He was known as Pastor Art to his congregation. He was fresh out of Bible college, young, and eager to bring souls to Jesus. He at least seemed to be willing to listen.

Unseasoned, not yet indoctrinated and cynical, he was willing to be wrong while searching for the truth. Art listened closely to Sean without interruption. Afterward, he did not offer the standard answers that Sean was used to hearing, or castigate him for believing in imaginary creatures. What he did promise was to investigate and pursue the matter. Finally, someone took the young man seriously, believed in him. Art asked Sean to try and draw pictures of the creatures but warned that he should keep them to himself. Sean quickly began to amass the rogue gallery of horror for their next discussion.

It was as if a huge weight had been lifted. Not that he expected that the creatures would somehow vanish, but that he had someone with whom he could share his fears. His mother and father attended church each Sunday, said and did all the right things, made friends and even joined in the culture of the church. Neither, however, pursued a relationship with Jesus, studied God's Word outside of the church walls, or made any attempt beyond church attendance. Sean, however, was drawn toward wanting to truly understand what Jesus was all about. Diligently he sketched his nightly horror, taking time to name and put a label on the recurring faces. Pastor Art's focus was on the older children, mostly the teens, but never failed to take time to counsel and meet with Sean.

It was just after he turned nine that his first physical assault came. Ador, a name given by Sean to the most dominant and largest of the demons, actually grasped his arm and pulled him from his bed. He felt the hands, cold and strong, as they closed around his wrists. The pain grew as the grip tightened, and he was catapulted across the room and into the wall. His scream awakened and brought his parents rushing into his room. They found him in tears, cowering against the wall, and holding his injured hand. Wide-eyed he told them of the encounter, but as always they accused him of having a nightmare, unwilling to consider any other possibility. Severe bruising on his arm the next morning failed to make them reconsider his claims.

However, when Pastor Art was shown the arm, he seemed honestly concerned and asked a lot of questions. Later when Sean showed him the sketches and pointed out Ador, Art became alarmed and made some photocopies. A week to the day it happened again, with Sean being slammed into the headboard of his bed. His head sported a bump and bruise that were noticed both at school and that night at the children's program. It was noted that both had happened on the night before his visits to the church. Just before the next meeting with Sean, Art brought the senior pastor into a private room where they stood looking at a large book and at Sean's drawings. Pastor Frank had a grave look when he walked over to Sean and sat down beside him.

"Sean, it is very important that you answer truthfully, do you understand?"

Sean nodded.

"Were your parents in the room when these two events happened?" Pastor Frank asked.

"No," he said. "The first time they came running in when I screamed. This last time I didn't wake them. They don't believe me anyway," he added.

"Are you sure?" he asked a second time, looking the boy directly in the eyes.

"I'm sure," Sean said.

Frank smiled. "I believe you," he said, "but we needed to be sure."

As Sean left he was plagued with uncertainty. What if he had dreamed it? What if his parents were right?

Sean had accepted Jesus when he was nine and had a keen appreciation for his Savior. Over time there had been a gradual lessening of the nightly terror that stalked him. But, it had never entirely gone away. Occasionally he'd see Ador's face in the reflection of a window. Each time when he looked around he'd find that Ador had disappeared. He had become accustomed to, but did not welcome, the presence that lay just beneath the surface of what others called reality.

~ ~

They were four to a room. The room was divided by a shared wall with two freshmen to each side. In the center each had an individual closet space and access to a shared bathroom. Many had showed up with everything they owned only to be then forced to send most of it back home. The rooms were just a step up from the cells the county provided to its inmates, but they were clean and sufficient for their purpose. Sean arrived, unlike most, with only a backpack and a single suitcase. He was looking forward to leaving home, making new friends, and preparing for whatever the future held. Sean was by nature an optimist, but a pessimist by experience, wanting to see the best in the world while at the same time realizing that the world held more pain and danger than joy. Casey shared a room with Sean. He was larger-than-life in every way. He was a full foot taller than Sean, nearly twice his weight, and speckled with freckles like a Dalmatian pup. Casey was on scholarship to play football for Boise State. He had moved down to the states from Moose Jaw, Saskatchewan. His campus visit was the first time he had ever been out of Canada.

The small university had risen to national prominence during the past several seasons by a program that boasted success without the large school trappings. The coaching staff had made it their forte to recruit gifted and hardworking athletes and make them into stars. They also seemed to care about their students' success in life after college.

At 165 pounds, Sean would be the lightest man on the team - that is, if he was able to make the team. He would try making a place for himself as a walk-on. He'd had notable success as a kicker in high school but had not been offered a scholarship. Casey was tall, strong, and fast on his feet. He had been the local star in the high school program. Now he was one of 23,000 students, each one looking for an edge.

When he and Casey walked into the athletic director's welcoming reception it was apparent that athletes came in all shapes and sizes. Tennis, track, football, basketball, swimming – the list went on and on. The reception hall held nearly four hundred prospective athletes, all eager to be considered for the various teams. The athletic director, university president, and coaches introduced themselves and welcomed the students to the university. After a substantial buffet meal the coaches retired to the nearby stations representing their sport. Prospects were urged to gather to the location of their choice for personal instruction. The head coach, flanked by several assistants, spoke briefly before inviting the students to return at a later time to demonstrate their prowess on the field. Casey, of course, would try out for the defensive or offensive line. Sean pinned his hopes on his foot.

It was nearly midnight when they returned to the dorm and after one when they finally finished visiting and drifted off to sleep. A heavy

thump and muffled scream awakened Sean. Across the room in the dim light he could see Ador holding Casey down, having pulled him from the bed to the floor. Casey's eyes were fixed on his attacker, terror written across his face.

Sean suddenly remembered a verse from his childhood, *He who is in me is greater than he who is in the world.*

This caused Ador to hiss and turn toward him. "And who is this He you are claiming to know?"

Sean had never heard his voice this clearly before and shrank back at the words. "He is Jesus, Son of God, my Lord and Master."

Ador, scoffed at first but a change became apparent in his serpentine eyes. Then, as if in a dream, he was gone.

It seemed strange to Sean to see a 300-pound giant lying on the floor with tears running down his cheeks, but there he was with eyes still wide with fear.

"What, what was that?" Casey asked as he moved to the edge of his bed.

"I call him Ador," Sean answered. He was pleased that someone else had finally seen him.

Casey looked shocked. "So, you know him? You've seen him before?"

"Yes, many times, but never with someone else in the room."

Sean felt relieved that he finally had someone to talk to about Ador, someone who actually knew that he existed. They dressed, left their room, and went to the coffee shop where they talked until the sun came up. When they returned to the room they found the other half of the room still asleep. Sean made a call to his hometown, catching Pastor Art still in bed. He had forgotten about the time difference and quickly apologized for waking him. It had been almost four years since they had last talked. At first Art didn't remember Sean. With the mention of Ador, Sean could tell he had gained his friend's attention.

Sean put Casey on the phone and said, "Tell him what you saw."

Casey reconstructed the event in vivid detail, bringing goose bumps to Sean's neck and forearms.

When Sean got the phone back, he asked, "So Art, what do we do now?" He could tell Art was unnerved when he said, "Give me your phone number and I'll get back to you."

~ ~

Demon possession and hauntings were the stuff that movies were made of, popularized by notable writers and actors. It was the big church that had the moxie to exorcise demons. It chose holy water, crucifixes, incantations, and ancient rituals read from great leather-bound books to try to address the issue. Even then priests often fell prey to the hands of evil. What did Sean have? All he had was his Bible and a Baptist pastor from small town USA. As he inventoried his assets, he seemed to come up short until he remembered what he had said that sent Ador scurrying. *He who is in me* ... The He is the Holy Spirit, who dwells within each believer. He felt strengthened but unaware of how one could fight a spiritual battle.

~ ~

Sean was asleep when the phone rang.

It was Art. "Everyone but Frank thinks we are both crazy," he said.

That news didn't sound very encouraging to Sean.

"Frank's retired now but seems interested. We are going to meet and discuss it at length. I'll get back to you."

At two o'clock they dressed down and assembled on the field for the first time with their prospective team. Both Casey and Sean were lacking the vigor they had hoped to show the coaches. Each man ran, did agility drills, threw and caught some balls, then settled down to their prospective positions. Casey was grunting and sweating with the line coaches while the defensive coach gave Sean a look in the secondary before letting him kick a few balls at the field goal. They had lunch in the cafeteria before returning to their room.

"Are you a Christian?" Sean asked his friend pointblank.

"I'm a Canadian," Casey answered with a smile. He then nodded his head yes.

"Have you ever had nightmares like the one we had the other night?"

Casey shook his head no.

"I wonder," Sean thought aloud, "why did he grab you rather than me?"

Casey laughed, a twinkle apparent in his blue eyes. "Maybe together we are a force to be reckoned with, eh."

The thought intrigued Sean. He jotted something down in his journal. Another elusive verse, teased him from years before, something about two strands being stronger than one. He made another note.

Sean knew that God was omnipresent, all knowing, unchanging, eternal, omnipotent, and more. He wondered about Satan and his lackeys. Could they know the future? Do they recognize a threat in advance? Had there been some reason why he had been singled out since childhood? And what of Molly, was she a part of this mystery? Was she alive somewhere? And what part did his new friend play in all this? Had God brought them together for a reason?

After a nap the two walked to the library where they spent the afternoon and most of the evening reading everything they could find on demon possession, powers and principalities, Satan, and Biblical accounts of dark angels. Most of it was of little value, some was outright fiction, and the rest just theory. That is until they opened a book with ancient illustrations. Both were stopped cold when a picture of Ador starred back at them from its pages. There was no doubt it was him. Sean remembered his own sketch from years before, and the look both pastors Frank and Art had when they had searched through a similar book. They had known even then that he was telling the truth, but hadn't known how to deal with it. Would they know now?

When Art called back, he had Frank join him on the line.

Sean was ready. "Can or does Satan know those who are, or will be, his adversaries?" he asked.

"Good question," Art replied. "I'm not sure of the answer. He seems to have some foreknowledge but how much and from what source isn't really clear. He may know some future details from what is written down in God's Word. According to the book of Acts his minions seemed to be assisting a fortuneteller. Beyond that I couldn't really say."

"So, why me?" Sean asked. "Why have I been chosen to receive his special attention?"

With the speakerphone on, Casey was able to listen in on the conversation. Art was silent, thoughtful.

"Maybe God told him like he did with Job," Casey said.

"Maybe it was not Satan but God who knows the plans He has for you and pointed them out to Satan," Pastor Art suggested.

"But what about me?" Casey asked. "Am I just an innocent bystander?"

They all laughed.

"Collateral damage you mean? I doubt it. No one picks on a 300-pound guy without a reason. It was more likely an attempt at intimidation. Deceit, intimidation and creating fear are among their most common tactics. Of course those tactics don't work very well against a person who knows the Scriptures and the power of God." Art said.

"Hello, Sean," Frank said. "It's been a long time."

"Yes sir, it has," Sean replied. "Why didn't you tell me that you recognized Ador from one of those pictures in the book on demons?"

"You were too young, son. And frankly we didn't know how to handle it.

"And do you know now?" Sean asked.

"No, well maybe. We are working on a theory.

"Can I ask you both a few questions?" Art asked.

"Go ahead," they said together.

"Are both of you are saved? You claim Jesus as your Redeemer, right?"

They answered affirmatively.

"Are you aware of any unconfessed sin in your life?"

"No."

"Have you knowingly participated in any cult ceremonies, witchcraft games, or given any spirits permission to control or influence you?"

"No."

"Good. What are your plans after college? Do you have any occupational plans? Entering the military, marriage, anything at all?"

Both boys felt embarrassed at their lack of plans.

"Ministry?" he asked.

"I have thought about it some." Casey replied. "My grandpa is a minister. I've always held that out as a possibility."

"How about you Sean?"

Sean smiled. "A missionary came to our church and talked about his work in Africa. Molly and I talked about wanting to do that some day."

"Bingo!" Frank said. "God lives in the past, present, and future, sees it all as one. He sees us as we will be in His plan for our lives. Just like when God proudly pointed out His servant Job, he may have done likewise with the three of you, and Satan took action to try to thwart the plan. But now it's coming together anyway, just as God planned.

Casey was excited. "Now that Sean and I are together we are stronger and better equipped."

Sean's smile faded. "But what about Molly? Wasn't she a part of it too?"

The line was quiet for a time.

"We are just speculating here. No man fully knows the mind of God," Art answered.

Frank changed the subject. "Why did you boys choose Boise State rather than Washington State or Oregon?"

Both seemed surprised.

"It was the only school who offered," Casey answered.

Sean smiled. "It was the only school I considered."

"So, maybe God narrowed down the field for you? Art asked.

Both boys replied, "Yes."

The four agreed to talk again the next day after church.

~ ~

As soon as the two clerics hung up the phone, they spent a good deal of time in prayer together asking for clarity, wisdom and direction. As they parted, Frank took time on the drive home to stop by the police station. Twelve years was a long time. The primary detective working on Molly's case had retired but his younger partner was still active.

Detective Masters was a balding man, in his 50s, overweight and overworked. He welcomed Frank, relieved for a break in the daily routine. "How may I help you, Pastor?"

"An old case, about twelve years ago, a missing girl."

"Molly, Molly Carpenter?" Masters asked with enthusiasm.

Frank nodded.

"She's been on my mind lately," Masters said. "I pulled the cold file just yesterday to give it a fresh look."

"Really?" Frank asked. "Why?"

"Don't know. It just struck me that I hadn't given it a look for a while."

"And?" Frank pressed. "Did you see anything new?"

Masters smiled. "Don't know for sure, but something struck me that we had never noticed before."

"What's that?"

"A sister, half-sister really. Mrs. Carpenter had a half-sister who lived in Richland. She was never married, had a baby out of wedlock. It died of SIDS shortly after birth. We never gave her much thought since she lived out of town. It just got me to wondering what became of her, so I ran a check. She and her child moved to Boise, Idaho, about twelve years ago. Hasn't been heard from since."

"Her child?" Frank said. "I thought you said her baby died."

"It did. I have the birth certificate and death certificate for Naomi Jones. I checked with the Ada County Sheriff and found her listed with a child."

"So, Naomi Jones is possibly a cover name for Molly Carpenter and is now about eighteen and living in Boise?"

"That's about it," Masters said, smiling. "I just put it together today. I haven't had a chance to follow it up with Boise P.D."

"I'd appreciate it if you'd keep me in the loop," Frank said. "I'm working with Molly's brother, Sean, who has just moved to Boise."

The detective gave him a quizzical look. "Just moved to Boise?"

"He's just beginning college there. I knew him as a child during the time of the kidnapping."

He was anxious to get home to give Art a call. This was one of the first times in his entire life when he wished he had a cell phone.

"Art?" he said into the phone. "I have just come from the police department." He continued to tell his friend about the entire conversation with detective Masters.

Art drew in his breath then spoke. "God does indeed work in mysterious ways. What do we do now?"

The line was silent for a time before Frank answered, "We pray for God's will to be done. It appears that His plan has been in the works for many years and is about to come to completion without our intervention."

~ ~

Sean lay awake running the events of the past three days over and over again in his mind. The illuminated dial on the bedside clock shone red, casting an eerie glow into the small room as the minutes continued to pass. Across the room Casey was lying motionless as well. His mind was cluttered with questions about the strange boy who shared not only the room with him, but who also seemed to be connected to him. Two fifty-nine, the exact same time he had been awakened over and over again. It seemed that after trying to stay awake for hours, when he was finally overcome by sleep he would always reawaken at two fifty-nine.

Suddenly he awoke to the smell of smoke. He wondered why there was no sound from the smoke alarm. As his eyes opened they focused first on the clock and then on the room behind it. Looming over him were yellow eyes filled with hate. It was the dark, shadowy figure of Ador, his foul breath threatening to suffocate him. He heard Casey making a sound reminiscent of a frightened child, but said nothing.

Did he actually hear Ador's words or did he just sense them, Sean wondered as the cold hands closed around his throat. He was paralyzed with fear, unable to scream, and hardly able to move as he fought to loosen the grip which threatened to crush his windpipe. It was useless. The hands were like iron. His efforts were futile as his body began to embrace the darkness of his own death.

He began to pray. "They overcame him by the blood of the lamb ..." Soon he lost the ability to concentrate as his body closed down.

From across the room came a cry of fear mixed with anger as Casey crashed into Ador with all of his might. For a moment Ador's grip loosened as he turned to meet his new foe. This allowed air into Sean's starving lungs.

Sean watched his friend being smashed against the wall like a blindsided quarterback. "God, help us," he prayed.

At once the room began to glow with a white light, which began at the floor and extended to the ceiling. It looked like brilliant particles of dust caught in sunlight. Within seconds the particles changed into a solid form, the shape of a man. He seemed too large to fit into the space, like his head might go through the roof as he continued to grow and expand. As Sean watched the ceiling disappeared, the evening stars formed a backdrop to the figure as it grew to a greater height. He seemed at once both nearby and far away, close at hand and remote, intimate but endless. Sean's mind registered all this in a split second as he regained his breath. Ador cowered before the majestic form. He was then crushed by one of the great, white hands. Peace came over the room, and a sense of comfort and serenity filled the young men.

The majestic form spoke into their hearts, "I know the plans I have for you, plans for good and not for evil."

It may have been a second, a minute, or an hour; but then it was gone. The light faded, the room darkened, and they were restored to their normal concept of reality. The room smelled fresh and clean. There was no cry from their neighbors, no evidence of it ever having happened except the hole in the sheet rock where Casey had caved it in.

The morning sun awakened the boys. It was nearly eight o'clock when they roused. They took turns in the shower without conversation. Sean gingerly touched his throat, feeling the tenderness and seeing the bruising in the mirror as he shaved and combed his hair. He could see a similar dark bruise on the arm and shoulder of his massive friend as he watched him pull on his shirt.

"How's the shoulder?" Sean asked, smiling at the Canadian.

Casey shrugged and smiled. "Better than your neck, eh?"

They walked across the campus comparing their memories of the night's events.

"Do you think it's gone?" Casey asked, referring to Ador.

"I do," Sean answered with more conviction than he actually felt. "Who do you think the big guy was?" he continued.

Casey was silent for a moment before he answered. "Jesus maybe, or at the very least an angel."

When they arrived at the campus church the music had already started. Most of the seats were already taken. The two men finally seated themselves in the front row. Sean didn't know Casey's religious upbringing but found the upbeat tempo of the worship and the energy around him uplifting. His eyes were drawn to the worship team, in particular to a petite, young woman who was singing backup. When the pastor took the podium the worship team took their seats in the audience.

Created for a Cause was the title the pastor had chosen for his message. It became clear that God had not just randomly created us, but had done so with a purpose.

Sean smiled and whispered to Casey, "We are not just off the rack. We are custom made."

The backup singer overheard his comment, smiled and nodded.

An hour later the service closed with a rock hymn unknown to Sean. The crowd soon began to file out, spreading out across the street and onto the campus.

"Several of us are meeting at the SUB for a bite to eat and to discuss the message. Do you want to join us?"

He almost ignored the comment, thinking the invitation was meant for someone else. When he stopped and turned he was looking into the hazel eyes of the brunette singer. To his relief, she repeated her invitation. Casey nodded.

"Thank you, we will," Sean said.

Nearly all of those gathered were freshmen, and most had only been on campus for a few days. Others were from the Campus Crusade and InterVarsity groups. They were Christian groups that met at the campus for fellowship. Sean and Casey were invited to a get acquainted event scheduled for later in the week. And that is how Sean met his sister again after twelve years.

"Sean Carpenter," he said taking her hand.

"Naomi Jones," she replied, looking directly into his eyes. "Have we met?"

There was a supernatural element to it all, something that transcended a physical attraction between a young man and woman, a bond. At first Sean dismissed it as just another pretty girl with a great personality and a good sense of humor. Although that was all true, there seemed to be something deeper, more significant about her. Casey had noticed it as well. She had an element of maturity and commitment that the others lacked.

At the dorm, Sean and Casey continued to discuss the all too real events of the prior night and the contrast to the morning's church service. The subject then turned to tomorrow's football practice. When the phone rang, it was Art with Frank in the background on speakerphone. Before the pastors could speak, both boys unloaded, telling in detail what they had experienced the previous night. It went on for some time, with each adding their own dimension to the story until finally they paused. There was a long silence causing Sean to wonder if they had lost the connection.

"You both saw and experienced the same miraculous event for the same purpose, His purpose," Frank said.

Art added, "We have something more to share with you about Molly."

"Now," Frank cautioned, "this is only speculation at this point. Detective Masters is yet to find anything concrete to support our theory."

It was Art and Frank's turn now to share their excitement with the boys. When they stopped talking the line went silent for a few seconds. Sean and Casey needed a little time to reflect on what they had just been told.

"I, we met her today," Sean said with a shaky voice. "I'm sure of it. She sat right beside me in church, and we visited afterward at the SUB. She introduced herself as Naomi Jones."

The men considered for a few moments the enormity of what they had just learned.

Finally Sean spoke. "What do I do? Should I go to her and tell her what we suspect? Blood tests would prove who she really is."

Frank spoke quietly but firmly. "Have you met your coach yet?"

"Yeah, we spent a few minutes with him yesterday," Sean said. "We have our first practice tomorrow."

"Did he say what his plans are for the season?" Frank continued.

"Well," Sean said, "not in detail. Just that he wants us to come together and operate as a team and do the best we can. He plans to win, I'm sure."

"So, he does have a plan for the team. And having just met him, how do you think he'd like it if you came in and tried to take over without knowing what that plan was? Do you think you could improve on his plan?"

"I get it," Sean said. "You don't think God needs our help do you?"

Both Frank and Art laughed.

"Son," Art said, "you are quicker than most. Most of us just jump in thinking somehow that God can't finish the job unless we help Him out. It's the same pride and ego that caused Satan to fall. We get a god complex and see ourselves as the answer to every question."

"So what do we do now?" Casey asked.

"Just show up for practice and see what the coach has in mind and then do it," Frank answered.

~ ~

Over the next week detective Masters made phone contact with the local police, sent them copies of the case file, and DNA samples. Behind the scenes Boise Police detectives did background checks on Beverly Jones and Naomi Jones. They elicited Naomi's address from her college registration. With a doctored copy of an Oregon birth certificate, Molly had entered the first grade as Naomi Jones. Her records subsequently had never again been questioned, being passed forward from grade to grade right up to her early graduation. Beverly had led an unremarkable life, never giving anyone reason to investigate or question her. Sean was having trouble keeping all the balls in the air, and his mind was having difficulty focusing on academics, football, his spiritual life, and especially Molly. Ador fortunately, had not returned.

When the Boise Police Department brought Beverly in for questioning, they had alerted detective Masters. He drove all the way to

Boise to sit in on the questioning. After at first denying the allegations, she later admitted her part and explained it away with what seemed like a fairy tale. At eighteen she had become pregnant. She was alone and unprepared to raise a child. One night she had been awakened by a noise from the baby's room. In the room, appearing like a dark shadow, someone or something was leaning over the child with its face pressed against it. When she awoke the following morning the baby was dead. She had been too frightened to tell the incredible story to anyone. Five years to the day, the skulking form returned carrying Molly under one grotesque arm with instructions for her to raise the child or she too would be killed. Again, the young woman had allowed the demon to rule her life. She was unknowingly filling the void in her heart with her niece. She had told Molly that bad men had killed her family and they needed to move away and hide from them.

Molly had never questioned the need to use another name and had eventually all but forgotten her early life. It was only recently that Jesus had become important to her again. God had impressed upon her a need to return and be faithful. Those emotions also brought with them a sense of loss and a longing to know more about her real family.

With input from trained psychologists much care and preparation preceded the reunion. Beverly explained the events to Molly just as she had to the detectives. The Carpenter family watched from another room. Then Sean joined them, with pastors Art and Frank, and he told his incredible saga. Finally her parents joined them amid tears of joy and expressions of forgiveness.

~ ~

After two years on a winning college football team, Casey transferred to a small Bible school in Montana, less than a day's drive from his home. He plans to pursue ministry as an evangelical missionary. Sean and Molly have become instrumental in the work of Campus Crusade and plan to be missionaries after graduation. Beverly underwent extensive mental health therapy and has returned to society complete, at peace, and forgiven by God and man. Mr. and Mrs. Carpenter accepted Jesus' salvation and are active in their church. God reigns and Jesus saves. Amen and Amen.

'For I know the plans that I have for you,' declares the LORD, 'plans for welfare and not for calamity to give you a future and a hope. 'Then you will call upon Me and come and pray to Me, and I will listen to you. Jeremiah 29:11,12   NASB

Rewind

"Just a little more," Josh said. "I'm almost there."

Above him his friend let a couple feet of line slip between his gloved hands before arresting it again.

"How's that?" Brett asked, leaning back against the strain of the rope.

"Good. Hold it there while I get a handhold," Josh answered. "The side shaft takes off here at a ninety-degree angle to the main one. It's about six or seven feet in diameter."

"You're down about ninety feet," Brett informed him. "What can you see?"

"Hardly a thing. The darkness soaks up this little LED like a dry sponge," Josh answered. "We'll need some real light down here when we get going. Hold on, I'm going to try and swing away from the wall and back a couple of times until I can get into the side shaft. There are no handholds to pull myself into it."

"Roger, got ya. Go ahead," Brett answered. "What kind of rock is down there?"

"Igneous," Josh replied. "I think the main shaft is natural, maybe a vent tube from a volcano or something. Smooth as glass, but the side one is definitely manmade. I can see tool marks around its circumference."

Brett nodded but did not answer.

"I'm in!" Josh declared triumphantly. "I'm standing in a horizontal tunnel. Give me some slack."

Brett obliged, playing out several feet before tying it back off.

"I'm going to unhook now and look around some. I'll use the big lantern and see how far it goes."

Brett was nervous. "Why don't you leave it on. I'll give you fifty feet or so and tie it off to the truck? If the floor gives way you may get hurt but not lost."

"Okay," Josh said. "Good plan. If I can get enough light I'll send you some pictures on my cell."

The pictures were ghastly, much like those on some television show about haunted houses. At least they gave Brett an idea of what his friend was seeing. Just the fact that Josh was standing up with some headroom gave him an idea of the size of the tunnel. There was no dirt - only a dark colored stone that resembled obsidian with a glasslike texture.

"Can you see the bottom of the main shaft?" Brett asked.

Josh hesitated, then said, "Nope, no chance. The darkness just seems to eat up the light."

"Drop a couple of chem lights and see what happens," Brett suggested.

"Good idea." A moment later he said, "Didn't work. I watched them until they disappeared. Never did see the bottom."

"Sucker's deep," Brett said in awe. "We are going to need a lot more gear when we come back." The last few feet of the line finally played out over the rim of the hole and then stopped. "You need more line?" Brett asked his friend. There was no response. Brett moved to the edge and shouted down into the shaft, repeating his question. Still no answer. The yawning blackness seemed to beckon him toward the hole. He grabbed the line and gave it three quick jerks. He felt no resistance as the line hung loosely in his hands. His repeated shouts into the hole yielded no response, causing him to choke with emotion.

He stood dumbfounded between the pickup and the edge of the hole, gazing down into its open mouth. There was no sound in the desert, not a bird, an animal, or the slightest hint of civilization. Brett felt as if he were the only living thing in the whole area. He was torn between leaving to go find help and staying nearby in case his friend might call out to him. Adding to the problem was the lack of anything nearby to secure the rope. If he disconnected the rope from the truck it would fall into the hole. If he pulled it up he would have no way to get it back into the horizontal shaft where his friend had apparently gone.

~ ~

They had found the hole quite by accident while still in high school. On that particular day they had been riding their dirt bikes and chasing coyotes across the high flat mesa when a large male coyote just disappeared in front of them. When they got to the spot where they lost sight of it, the hole seemed to still be licking its chops, having devoured the coyote without leaving a sign. Now years later, having rafted the class IV rapids of the Northwest whitewater rivers, climbed the rock faces of the Rocky Mountain cliffs, and survived three weeks in the jungles of South America, the hole had seemed a small challenge in the overall scheme of things. Perhaps, Brett thought, they had underrated it simply because it was such an innocuous hometown kind of thing.

~

Darkness was nearly upon him when he finally pounded the tire iron into the ground and tied off the rope. He knew that even driven eighteen inches into the hard ground the iron may only give Josh a false sense of security if he tried to use it to climb out. It very likely would not support his weight all the way out of the hole, dropping him to his death when it pulled free. On the other hand, the rope was his only hope of finding his friend when he returned.

He had just gotten into the pickup and hit the starter when the headlamps silhouetted what at first appeared to be an oversized bat emerging from the mouth of the cavern. It was there and gone before he could focus his attention. Out of the ground, into the beams of the halogen lights, then up into the waiting darkness it flew without a sound. Brett turned off the ignition and sat back recounting the event, questioning his eyes and his mind. Did he see something? How large was it? What was it? Was it even real or just his imagination?

He knew he had seen something. As he thought back, he remembered that the object had been framed between the headlamps. The headlamps in turn showed only the edges of the hole. He calculated the distance to the hole, the six feet between the lamps, and the diameter of the opening and came up with a figure of fifteen to eighteen feet. The very idea of a bat with a fifteen-foot wingspan caused him to rethink his math. Was he dreaming or was it possible?

~ ~

He followed the pickup's tracks back across the desert and finally to the paved roadway leading to town. His mind was running wild as he considered the possibilities. No indigenous bird had a wingspan in excess of ten feet and none of the larger birds lived below ground. It seemed to unfurl its wings once above the opening, begging the question as to how it got to the top of the tunnel. Brett recalled his last viewing of the movie Jurassic Park and the pterodactyls flying over the canyons. He wondered if this may be a possible descendant.

Brett finally made it home, a small house he shared with Josh. Once inside he popped open a Coke, grabbed a pad and pen, and began to make a list of supplies – climbing gear, food, medical supplies, water, signal flares, lightweight sleeping sacks, gloves, a backboard, pulleys, body armor, headlamps, and spare batteries. His .357 Ruger, shoulder holster and a box of ammo rounded out the equipment list. Outside Josh's Jeep CJ7 was parked beside the garage. He jumped in, backed it close to the door, and began to load up. He checked the two GI cans on the rear bumper and found them full of gas. He was nearly loaded when he remembered he needed to get the tie downs from the garage. Inside the garage he grabbed half a dozen spikes, used in concrete forming, and a wood-splitting maul.

"Think," he said to himself as he started the restored Jeep. "What are you forgetting?"

~ ~

He was just turning off the blacktop onto the desert when he remembered he had left his cell phone in the truck.

Overhead the stars twinkled brightly in the cloudless sky, appreciating the fact that no artificial light competed with their beauty. The moon was just a sliver and lent little light to the scene, making it necessary to use Josh's light bar to show the way. By eleven thirty Brett had found the hole and began unpacking the gear. Having hurriedly unpacked he surveyed the assembled equipment with satisfaction before realizing that what he really needed was another person to attempt a rescue. Once he started the descent, he knew there was a good chance neither of them would ever see the surface alive. He approached the hole, directed his million candlepower light into it, and yelled to his friend. He waited a few minutes before repeating the futile gesture. He then slipped into a sleeping bag to await the coming dawn.

As he slept he was troubled with the howls of wolves and red eyes peering at him in the darkness. He heard the rustling of dry leaves and smelled the foul breath of a rotting corpse trying to communicate with him in his dreams. He awoke with a cold, dry sweat on his body. He seemed to linger somewhere between slumber and consciousness in what old television shows had called the twilight zone. He lay shivering until the first rays of light broke in the east, then shed his artificial cocoon and began to formulate a plan for his friend's rescue.

Unhooking the A-frame tow bar from its upright position and lowering it nearly horizontal, he tied it securely to the Jeep's roll bar for support. He attached a carabiner and an open pulley to its prominent point to accept the cable from the Jeep's winch. The spool on the winch read one hundred feet with a maximum load of 2,000 pounds. That gave him some confidence. He shortened the line around the roll bar and lifted the A-frame to a forty-five degree angle so that he could position the backboard beneath it.

With the sun's arrival he repacked the backboard with equipment, secured the line taken from the tire iron to the front bumper and another like it to the opposite side, then got down on his knees and began to pray.

"What are you doing?" came a voice sounding like rushing floodwaters. "You have no place here."

Brett looked up. The sunrise seemed to give a red glow to the eyes of the nearly featureless face looking down on him. Brett was startled that there had been no sound when the figure approached. It stood between him and the edge of the hole. It was wrapped in what appeared to be a black leather duster of the kind used by horsemen during inclement weather. The figure loomed above him menacingly for the few seconds it took him to gain his composure and reply.

"I am here to help a friend who has gone down in the hole behind you," Brett said. "He may be hurt or worse. I am waiting for the light so I can go down and find out."

"Neither you nor your friend belong here," the shadowy figure repeated his challenge. "You'd do well to leave him to his fate and go."

Brett heard a rustling of leaves, vividly bringing back to memory his dreams of the past night. It seemed to come from the movement of the strange dark figure. His visitor seemed to grow proportionately as Brett stood, appearing to leave little change in the relationship of their height. The more Brett tried to focus on the face before him the less distinct its features became. All at once, without a word, the figure seemed to step back and disappear down the yawning jaw of the hole.

Brett was visibly shaken by the ordeal, wondering if he was still dreaming, or dreaming again as he stood alone in the desert. How he wished that he had brought his cell phone or had stopped by the police station and given them a heads up. But now he felt it was too late. His only option was to attempt to rescue his friend.

He prayed again. "God help us."

~ ~

Josh and Brett had met in grade school, living beside one another until the sixth grade when Brett's parents had sold their home and moved a few blocks away. The distance had not affected their friendship except to make them use their bicycles in order to meet at one house or the other. They were like brothers and treated as such by both sets of parents. Josh's father was a minister at the Alliance church where Brett's family regularly attended. Both Brett and Josh felt the call to salvation at age thirteen while at church camp. They had committed their lives to Jesus around the same campfire one warm August evening.

~ ~

The idea of abandoning Josh had never been an option to Brett, even when his strange visitor suggested it. Even so, he knew that having another hand to remain topside would have been a prudent choice. He pulled the Jeep forward until the A-frame stuck out over the hole. He then placed rocks behind all four wheels and set the brake.

Trepidation, a word he had only heard in a Christian context, was the term that best described how he felt. He began to unwind and lower the backboard and its contents. It would take most of the one hundred feet of cable to get the supplies to the approximate depth. The weight of the gear was showing a noticeable strain on the roll bar, so Brett tied another rope from it over the back to the trailer hitch for safety's sake. He then double-checked his knots and started repelling into the darkness. As he began to descend he told himself it was just like coming down the face of a cliff, which he had done many times. But somehow it felt different in the darkness.

Just as Josh had described, the headlamp was of little use except to illuminate his hands and his climbing gear as he worked the line through the rings, which allowed him a gradual descent. The air seemed heavy and stale. As he breathed, his nostrils detected the stench of decay and death that had been so vivid in his dream. He looked below and saw nothing but the steel cable trailing off into the darkness. As he continued to look, small red dots appeared far below resembling tiny red stars in a distant sky. Brett closed his eyes. When he reopened them the spots were gone. He checked his watch. It was seven fifteen when he first touched the backboard and began looking for the side tunnel with the big light. The cavern walls resembled pottery that had been fired in a kiln, having a smooth, glazed appearance to them. Brett supposed that volcanic heat had caused its surface to become smooth long after the original vent tube had cooled.

Josh's line stopped its downward journey and turned into the mouth of a manmade lateral. Brett followed it in and turned on his big light to illuminate the cavern. With some difficulty, Brett drove an anchor into the wall and tied off Josh's rope, pulling the backboard toward him and tying it off as well. He carefully unpacked many of the supplies and left them in the entrance of the side tunnel.

In addition to the anxiety which heightened his fear, he now also felt the weight of separation and hopelessness. It pressed from every side attempting to crush his spirit and dissolve his will. Brett needed to focus. As he did, bits of Scripture came to mind independent of one another, like scraps of food to a starving man. Finally his mind calmed and his resolve returned. His need to find his friend once again became his mission. Brett set off into the tunnel holding Josh's original line. He counted his steps as he went and was thirty paces in when the line came to an end. He tied another line to it and then continued to count as he followed the tunnel in and gradually downward.

"I can do all things through Christ who strengthens me," Brett repeated over and over.

Operating with just the headlamp, attempting to save the big light for later, he had to overcome the urge to panic and run into the blackness that robbed him of his senses.

"He did not cast me out, you know," a soft voice came from somewhere in the darkness. "I chose to leave, and many chose to leave with me. You foolish ones choose to believe the story He has told, never questioning its truth."

Brett froze. Had he heard a voice, or was he imagining it here in this hellhole? "Who are you?" Brett asked, hoping to receive no answer.

"You know that," the smug reply came. "You have always known me. You knew me first, before He told you lies and took you away from me. You knew me well and walked with me each day until you turned thirteen and abandoned me."

"What is your name?" Brett asked. "Are you real? Am I dreaming again?"

"Have we been so long apart that you have forgotten me? I am always with you, always waiting to accept you back if you renounce the One who has given you empty promises. I deliver when I promise, here and now, today when you need it, not maybe somewhere and someday after you die."

Brett could see the red eyes, could smell the acrid breath, which seemed nearer now.

"Test me and see if what I say is not true," he challenged. "Is it not true that death comes to both the rich and the poor? Aren't both the wicked and the just treated equally on earth? Do only those who believe His lies find wealth and power? No! I am the one who treats everyone equally. I don't make impossible demands that none can keep. He threw them out of His garden and shut the gate. Only I followed."

Brett listened and felt himself being drawn in to the web being spun around him. "Where is Josh?" he asked the blackness.

"He is here with us. He has chosen to remain with me."

"Liar, Deceiver!" Brett said. "Josh has chosen the light and not the darkness, and Jesus as his Lord and Master."

A laugh filled the tunnel. "Has he? Has he now? Why don't you ask him whom he has chosen?"

The tunnel was filled with a reddish glow that seemed to pour through the walls. Just ahead of him Brett was able to make out the silhouette of his friend.

"Josh, is that you?" Brett asked, "Are you all right?"

"I'm fine," Josh said. His voice sounded detached. "Why are you here?"

"I am here to help you, to rescue you," Brett said.

"I don't need your help. I don't need saving," Josh answered. "Go home and forget me."

Another laugh filled the cavern. "Didn't I tell you? He's happy here. He wants to stay with me."

Our Father who art in heaven, hollowed be Thy name ..., Brett began in his mind.

The red glow faded and went out.

"Foolish one," the cackled reply came. "Do you think you can stand against me?"

Brett continued without answering. *Lead us not into temptation, but deliver us from...*

The sound of dry leaves blowing in the wind, of a thousand wings beating against restraint, filled the tunnel and blotted out his words.

... for Thine is the kingdom, and the power ..., he recited, trying hard to focus in spite of the noise and activity all around him.

Brett went to Josh, folded his arms around his friend, and held him close, then quoted Jesus saying, "I will never leave you nor forsake you."

"You'll die," the shrieked threat came out of the darkness. "You'll both die here, and no one will ever know. Others have before you."

"Yea though we walk through the valley of the shadow ...," Brent recited with Josh following his lead, "we will fear no evil."

~ ~

"What do you think," Josh asked as they sat at the table eating. "Shall we get up early tomorrow and see if we can find that hole in the desert again? We can take our gear and climb down and see what's in it."

"You mean the one we found when we were riding our bikes and chasing coyotes?" Brett answered."

"Yeah, that's the one. I always wondered what was in it. Maybe it's time to find out."

"No," Brett answered, "probably nothing down there but dead coyotes and rabbits. Besides, we promised to help Mrs. Gray rake leaves tomorrow, and she needs our help."

Significant Works

It was the lowly straw mixed with Egyptian clay that made the bricks durable. Today it is the grains of sand that give mortar its enduring strength. What is it that brings meaning and significance to what we do? Perhaps it will be a single, heroic act, giving our life for another. More likely it will be a series of small, ostensibly unselfish acts that will lead to the words, "Well done, good and faithful servant." Her contribution involved not a single decision to do something momentous but a lifetime of choosing to live in God's light and walking in His strength and power.

~ ~

She walked slowly. The arthritis created pain with every step she took. Her back curved in a perpetual forward lean, making her look several inches shorter than her original five feet. Her auburn hair had long been replaced by gray, then again by white. Her once clear, hazel eyes were shrouded by cataracts allowing very little light to come through their clouded lenses. She endured when others had given up. She lived on because there was still work to be done. There were times when she longed to leave the world behind. To see her husband, friends, and family once again would be inexplicable joy. To spend eternity with her Savior was her greatest ambition.

Her mind remained relatively clear. She knew how truly blessed she was, for so many had lost connection with the present and lived only in the past. She did not have the normal duties associated with children, then grandchildren, and now great-grandchildren. No, her task was not the daily chores of cooking and cleaning for them, helping with homework, and answering endless questions. That was the work of their parents. Her single focus was on prayer. Prayer unceasing as the Word of God plainly recorded it. There remained in her aged body little stamina or vitality for the world's labors. Getting dressed and feeding herself were more than enough to drain her waning energy. It was as she bowed her head and called out to her faithful Friend that she became empowered, gaining new strength and conviction with each word. At these times she felt no pain - only a renewing of her spirit, youthful vigor, and clarity of purpose coursing through her veins. The face of these children filled her memory with their uniqueness, their individual needs and trials, and her own hopes for their future. She prayed not as many do, but as friends speak to one another without reservation or motive, with openness and honesty.

She knew the many facets of prayer quite well. Like an expertly cut gemstone, her prayers revealed the Light of the World if one would take time to see. She did not like to think of her prayer time as dedicated, but dedicated it was nonetheless. She'd rather think of it as reserved, time set aside for the important work it was. She knew without a doubt that each prayer would be heard and properly answered in God's own time. Sometimes she felt God chuckle along with her when she pushed Him to answer her urgently felt requests.

She had been born with an intelligent mind, but more importantly over the years she had gained wisdom. She was well aware that knowledge can be gained through effort, but wisdom was a gift from God. She prayed that some of what she had learned could help others and provide a legacy lasting long after she had gone home.

~ ~

Running across the field sprinkled with wildflowers, jumping to catch a butterfly, rousing a fowl from its nest in a flutter of wings – these are the days of a young girl's life. There were things to be seen, lessons to be learned, and adventures to be taken. The life of a child, a pearl in the oyster of life. One of innocence and wonder, without pain or responsibility, life the way God had intended it.

They lived on a small farm down a long, dusty and rutted road several miles from a village. The date was July 1, 1925. A tiny, whitewashed house with a high-pitched roof sheltered seven from both the winter's cold and summer's heat. The sixty acres around it were as flat as the kitchen table that occupied one of the three rooms. A back porch had been added but was yet to be screened in. The attic had been roughly floored to provide room for the boys' beds. Father, as they reverently called him, had installed a staircase on the outside of the house for access. Three of the four boys slept in the two double beds on the porch during the late spring, summer and early fall, retiring to the attic during the winter. The youngest boy was still in a crib. It was kept in the room where the family's extra clothing, blankets, home canned food, and other treasures were stored. She slept with her parents in the big bedroom.

Out back, fifteen quick steps from the rear door, was an outhouse, which served the family well. Beyond it was a lean-to they called the barn. The barn existed because they had need of a cow for milk and horses to work the land. It was functional but hardly sound, creaking and leaning away from any wind that blew. In the winter a rope led from the house to the outhouse and then to the barn so they could find their way in a blizzard.

The value of the small farm centered on the natural stream that provided life-giving water eight months of the year. Without it, they'd have been at the mercy of the weather. Father had enhanced a low land, forming dikes that allowed them to accumulate water to hold in reserve when demand was high and water was scarce. The little pond was the center of the children's recreation, a place to swim and catch frogs when warm and a place to try out their ice skates when the weather turned cold.

It was a time of rest for the nation, a time of peace between wars, and a time of plenty with no knowledge of the Great Depression that was looming ahead. Although the days were long and demanding they passed by predictably and pleasantly for the family. Father often read well-worn books to the family by the light of oil lamps. Of course, the Good Book was a daily feature. The older children had heard the stories so many times they could easily recite them from memory. They enjoyed hearing them nonetheless. They worked six days as Scripture dictated, then rested on Sunday, their Sabbath. Sunday gave reason to give thanks. They gave thanks for their health, for what they had, and for what they did not have.

Baptist, the family proudly answered the oft-asked question, although the small church had no denominational markings. Bap-tist, with emphasis on the "p" is how little Evelyn pronounced it.

The preacher, unable to garner adequate support from his small flock, worked during the week as a typesetter for the local newspaper. As a perk of the job the owner let him print the necessary church letters and bulletins in his off time.

Twenty-five was the usual number of seats filled on any given Sunday morning, with over half of them being children. Evelyn liked church. It gave her time to be with other girls her own age. She missed female companionship during the summer, surrounded by brothers who had no interest in dolls or girlie things. Her mother, her only ally, was often too busy to sit down with her for any length of time. That made her Sunday school time very special to her.

She was born six years after the end of the war and America had healed for the most part from the scars. It was a time of self-indulgence and immorality in the big cities, the nation having adopted a laissez-faire attitude about life in general. Some might call it the beginning of the decay of American morals. In the central states the attitude was less pervasive, or so it seemed in the rural farming community where they lived. They had enjoyed two years of back-to-back bumper crops, which allowed them to bring electricity to the farm and put a pitcher pump inside the house. In the second year they purchased their first automobile.

~ ~

It was the winter of 1928 when her brother John took sick and died from the effects of a ruptured appendix. By the time they had finally taken him to the doctor the infection had already overcome his little body. Evelyn had felt the closest to him and grieved his loss the most. It was in his honor, years later, that she named her own firstborn after him. Her oldest brother, Mahlon, had graduated from the eighth grade, moved into town, and had gotten a job at the mill. That left Albert, now fourteen, at home to help Father farm the land. Evelyn was learning how to bake, clean, and help her mother with the laundry. It fell to Jacob to pick up where Albert had left off, feeding the livestock and making sure they had firewood for the stove. Winter was particularly cold that year and made life more difficult than usual. Spring was a long time coming.

There had been over ten years of prosperity following the war, but in the fall of 1929 the bubble burst in America first and then spread across the world. Overnight it seemed the economy crashed and disappeared, and though it hardly seemed like it, the family was fortunate to be farmers. The farming community was as close as it came to being self-sufficient in a world turned upside down. The industrial revolution that had provided jobs and promise of a bright future for its workers quickly failed with unemployment rising above twenty-five percent. Mahlon returned home, jobless, to help on the farm.

Larger farms that had been converted to mechanical means of farming, or those with expansion debt or assets in failed banks, often lost everything. They watched as lifelong neighbors lost their homes and left on the road with all they owned on their backs. Though they tried, the church was unable to fully meet the staggering needs. The government aid kept folks alive but stole away dignity and hope. As always, some became wealthy at the expense of others and fortunes were made overnight. Their family was frugal and wisely had not gone into debt during the time of prosperity. Their father's wisdom had allowed them to survive when others had failed. In hindsight it seemed to Evelyn much like the story of Joseph in Egypt where the seven years of plenty were followed by seven of famine. There was little difference here except the time period was ten years.

~ ~

In 1939 the economy had started to turn around. Once again on December 11, 1941, war changed everything in America. The industrial machine cranked up, putting thousands back to work and uniting America in support of a cause. Evelyn had just turned sixteen and was entering high school when war was declared. Her two older brothers, Mahlon and Albert, joined the Army, which left only Evelyn and Jacob at home to help her parents run the farm. Jacob had wanted to join also, but her father's health was declining badly, forcing him to remain at home.

Evelyn had watched her world go from horses and buggies to cars and airplanes. Still the farm remained the staple in their lives. It provided both food and enough income to survive. She was able to complete high school while working in the war effort. Nearly everyone she knew made some contribution to the common cause as America fought her enemies valiantly.

When the letter came in January of 1944, it stated that Albert had been badly wounded at Anzio. The family was devastated but remained strong in their faith. Little had been heard from Mahlon who was to take part a few months later in the invasion at Normandy. There was pride in knowing that many of the crops from their farm and others like it were providing for the needs of those fighting overseas. Evelyn daydreamed that the very corn they grew would soon be filling the stomach of her brothers, that the wheat would be ground and become bread for their table, and that somehow they would know it was from the very farm where they had grown up. It was three more months before Albert got off the train. His shirtsleeve was neatly folded and pinned where his left arm should have been. He looked and walked like Father, old and tired.

As difficult as it had been to see their son and brother forever changed both physically and emotionally, it was worse when word came that Mahlon had not survived the landing at Omaha beach. Apparently he'd been killed as the first troops landed, only to be followed then by hundreds more as the Germans fought to repel their assault. Evelyn and Albert had not been close while growing up. But now with the losses of both John and Mahlon the family circle became smaller, closer, and each member more dear to one another. Father was diagnosed with a lung disease caused by the repeated assault upon his lungs by dirt and dust from the crops and fields. He became weak and frail almost overnight, forced to remain inside, usually wrapped in a blanket for warmth. He died peacefully in January of 1950 in the rocking chair he had made for his wife so many years before.

His passing removed the vitality and spunk of her mother, making her seem to age quickly. She too turned frail, depending more and more upon Evelyn and her sons for her needs. By summer, she too was gone. She had slipped quietly into forever sometime during the night just before her 52nd birthday. Jacob seemed fitted both by training and inclination to take over the farm. That fall he married a young woman named Carolyn and she moved onto the farm with him. Albert had since moved to Omaha and entered Bible college. As a disabled veteran the GI bill helped him get support for his education. His goal was to become a clergyman, but also gain the skills necessary to become an accountant. Evelyn met a young man that had returned from time spent in the Navy. They married and moved west to find their fortune together.

They seemed to be polar opposites. He was tall and quiet, she petite and outgoing. They began a family that same year after settling down in a small town in Idaho. He learned a trade as a baker working nights while going to school to become a teacher. Their first son, John, was born in the spring and their second a year later. They had a small farm on the outskirts of town, just a few acres with a couple of cows, chickens, and a large garden that kept Evelyn and their growing family busy. Soon he was teaching school full time. When their third son was on his way they struggled to make ends meet.

Though he had initially not attended church, Evelyn's Christian influence soon prevailed, causing her husband, and one by one her children, to find Jesus. They became active members at their little community church. Evelyn began attending a Bible study in an effort to satisfy her hunger for the Lord. "On fire" is the term many use when a believer has been touched in such a way as to be consumed with the pursuit of Jesus. She was indeed on fire – learning, teaching, and serving the Lord on every occasion and in every venue. Her husband was more reserved but no less committed to his faith, providing a guiding hand to his sons and Christian leadership to the family. Kathleen came much as Evelyn's younger brother John had, as a late but pleasant surprise. They had all but given up on having a daughter.

Paint us a picture if you will, a picture of joy and happiness, with no lack of pain and trials but with enough love to overcome them. I cannot, but yet God did, as He always does for His faithful ones. The family, now six, prospered…not financially, but in every other way. There was seldom surplus, but always enough. Isn't that after all what God has promised? Enough. And when there was surplus, isn't there always another in need? They were generous, giving, helping, loving and caring for those deemed less blessed than themselves. It became a way of life for the family, even the sons often coming home from school championing a need that they might meet.

As it is with man, time moves forward quietly yet relentlessly toward the eternal promise. One day it seems we are young and the next we are old. Her husband went to be with his Father far too early; or so it seemed for those who loved him on earth. Leaving behind a legacy of love, three sons, a daughter, a loving wife, and a life well lived. As his spirit rose to join Jesus in heaven he was given opportunity to reunite with those gone before where he waits patiently for those yet to come. And so the story continues, his children married, their children as well, and now their children's children.

One might wonder when she walks the earth which is not her real home: Are there those unknown who walk beside her, guiding her footsteps, bearing her aged body up, and giving clarity of purpose still as her mind begins to fail? "Unseen angels are proud to walk beside, before and after, this woman of grace and conscience who labors still to perform "works of significance!"

God's Provision

"Don't stop!" she said. "You never know when someone might have a gun or a knife and be waiting for an opportunity to hurt someone. Let someone else help them. Besides, we are already late."

"Late for what?" he answered, musing at her fear. He wondered when she had become so distrusting and cynical. "You wait inside and lock the doors. I'll just see if they need help."

He pulled their van onto the shoulder of the interstate several car lengths behind the stopped vehicle whose flashers were blinking weakly. As he stepped from the car, two semis and a group of cars passed without slowing.

The gray, overcast sky caused the figure standing by the car to blend into the bleakness of the flat desert scene.

"Afternoon, you need help?"

As the distance between them closed, Ken could see an aged man standing near the back of the car.

"I reckon we do. I was trying to make it to Buhl, but it looks like I underestimated how far I could get on empty. You ain't drivin' a fuel truck are ya?" he asked with a chuckle.

"Afraid not," Ken answered. "You got someone coming? Did you call for help?"

"Nah, we don't have none of those fancy portable phones. Besides, got no one to call," he said. "Was hoping a state trooper might stop and save us from spending the night."

"You're not alone then?" Ken inquired.

"Nah, the missus is inside keepin' warm. She's not well and the cold bothers her more than me."

Ken thought the man looked like something right off the cover of a Louis L'Amour book. He was about five foot nothin', as Louie would have told it, and about as heavy as a bag 'o them Idaho spuds. He had on the whole "getup," as they say: the worn out denim jeans, the big belt buckle, and a couple of spindly bowed legs that trailed off into pointy-toed boots. His western-cut shirt was long sleeved and buttoned to his chin and a farmer's hat covered his nearly bald pate.

"Name's Don," the man said, sticking out his hand. "Thanks for stoppin'."

Ken took the weathered hand in his and noted that it felt hard and calloused from years of hard work.

"Ken," he said back. "Ken Rydell. Glad to meet you."

"Where you headed, Ken?" the older man asked.

"My wife and I are headed to Twin Falls to see our new grandson," he said proudly. "Our daughter and her husband live there."

"First one, I 'spect," Don observed. "You don't look hardly old enough to have any yet. We got kids ourselves, but they're older 'n you."

"Let's walk back and see if we can rearrange our load a little and fit you both in," Ken said. "Our rig is about full. We're taking a load of baby stuff to the kids."

Ken could see his wife's displeasure written across her face as they approached.

"They're out of gas, and his wife's not well. I told him we'd make room and get them down the road," he said, as he opened the side door of the Rendezvous.

April didn't answer. He could feel her bristle at the delay. The seats had been folded down to allow for the big box with the crib in it, along with several boxes of clothes and toys.

"The big box might fit on top," Don offered, pointing to the luggage rack. "I think I got a length of rope in my rig."

"Good idea," Ken answered. "Bring the missus back with you and we'll get her warmed up and comfortable."

As the man returned to his old Chevy, Ken's wife turned on him and said, "You are going to mess around, and we'll be late for dinner with the kids. They had reservations you know."

"Give them a call and explain the situation. Tell them we'll be a few minutes late," Ken answered, trying to keep an edge out of his voice.

Up ahead they could see the old man open the trunk and take out a wheelchair, a blanket, and a length of rope before moving toward the passenger side of the car. Ken lifted the large box onto the luggage rack and snapped the seats into their upright position. It was just about a toss-up as to which was the weaker, Ken thought, as he watched the man help his wife from the car and into the wheelchair. He was painstakingly slow as he covered her with the blanket, turned the chair around, and locked the doors of the disabled car. It took several minutes to get her into the van, tie down the crib box, and find room for the wheelchair.

"Mighty nice of you folks to take the time to stop and help us," Ina said. "Lot of folks are in such a hurry these days. Boy, that heater sure feels good. I can't abide the cold since I started chemo a while back."

Don straightened her blanket as they pulled onto the highway.

"Yep," he echoed her sentiments, "sure is nice to be gettin' on home. I'm glad it's not outta your way much going down through the canyon instead of the highway."

"You folks live in Buhl for a while?" Ken asked.

"Most our lives," Don answered. "We moved there from Twin Falls after the war. We had a little dairy farm where we raised our children and scratched out a livin' before we retired."

Ken had not planned the side trip. He had just expected to drop them off where they could get fuel until he had seen the frail woman in the wheelchair.

"It won't take but a few minutes extra, and you can go back tomorrow with help to get your car," Ken said. He gave his wife a sidewise glance but didn't wait for her agreement.

"Funny how the Lord brings His people together in just the right way and at just the right times," Don said. "Yeah, He has a real way of makin' bad things into good ones."

As Ken looked in the mirror he could see that Ina had laid her head back against the seat and closed her eyes. He secretly wondered what good could come from this poor woman's suffering. "Do you come to Boise often?" Ken asked over his shoulder.

Don pulled himself forward with the help of the front seat and spoke quietly, "For a couple of months now we have been going every two weeks to the Mountain States Tumor Institute. It seems to be holding the wolf at bay, but not much more. It knocks her down for a few days. About the time she's back to herself, it's time to go again."

Ken was at a loss as to how he should respond.

"Funny thing is, in all those trips we always made it down and back on a tank of gas. We never did have to buy any along the way."

Ahead, Ken could see the flashing lights of emergency vehicles and road flares directing traffic onto the shoulder and around the scene of a major accident. Just beyond was the exit that would take them down into the canyon, along the Snake River, and up the little valley. Ken slowed, then stopped beside a state patrolman who was directing traffic

"What happened?" he asked.

"Lucky thing you weren't a few minutes earlier," the man in blue commented. "A car was in a hurry and cut off one of those big rigs," he said, pointing to a semi blocking the road. "The other semi tried to correct but was too late and hit them both." "We have serious injuries and several casualties."

Ken resumed his slow progress toward the exit ahead. "Maybe we know why you ran out of gas this trip," he said. "Or maybe we'll always wonder where we all would have been if you hadn't been forced to stop."

Next to him in the front seat, April was crying softly. Her hands were pressed to her face. Finally when her tears subsided, she attempted to wipe her moist, red eyes. Looking at her husband, she said, "The Lord works in mysterious ways." Then she quoted from the Bible, "Blessed be the Name of the Lord."

"Amen," came the muted response from Ina in the rear seat. "He seems to have provided for each of us."

The Nature of the Beast

Bob knew he shouldn't be doing business with them and that their reputation was well earned. Still he told himself, *I am short of money and know I can get a good deal. Besides, everyone else does it. It is okay if you don't know for sure that their merchandise is stolen, or that since it is already stolen you did not facilitate the theft.*

At least Al knew who he was and where he stood. He was a crook, a small-time thief of opportunity, and a man who had long ago strangled his conscience with a big wad of cash. He saw himself not much different than the CEOs who would sell off assets and bankrupt the company before jumping out with their golden parachutes. Or the Wall Street cutthroats that would raid a pension fund without a thought of the graying heads depending on it. What made him different was that he admitted it. He once had given a good laugh to a car salesman who forced him to fill out a credit application before test-driving a new car. Under occupation he had written "crook." He knew that putting it in writing didn't make it a lie even if others assumed it was a joke.

Al and his two brothers were from a long line of criminals dating back to moonshine and the prohibition era. He couldn't recall anyone on either side of the family tree who had ever worked a regular job. As a matter of fact he had heard of a couple of cattle rustling great-uncles who had swung from a crooked tree.

"Whatcha need?" Al asked the yuppie-lookin' man standing on his front step.

Bob swallowed and said, "I heard you might have a good deal on an amplifier."

"Heard where?" was the terse reply.

"Around. Some of the guys I play with recommended you."

"They got names?" Al continued, watching sweat begin to run into the collar of the yuppie's shirt.

"Lead guitar is Brad, and the drummer is Carl something," Bob said.

"What's the name of the group?" Al asked, having fun watching the kid squirm.

"Tenderfoot," Bob said, feeling satisfaction at knowing the answer.

"How come you don't know the names of the guys that you play with?" Al asked, holding the door only partly open.

"I just started playing with them," Bob said. "I'm new to town, and they needed a bass."

"What kind of bass?" he asked.

"An old Gibson," Bob said proudly.

"How much you lookin' to spend?"

"Not much. I don't have much cash. I just started a job."

"What do you do? Where do you work when you are not playing bass for the big timers?"

"Just started at the Exxon station, on Main, working nights until something better comes along.

"Now you are talkin'. A job with real promise. What brand you want?"

"I'd like to have a Marshall, but a Fender would do."

"Yeah, I'll bet it would," Al laughed. "I'll bet it would."

"Do you have one for sale? Anything in stock?"

"What do you think this is, Wal-Mart? We keep our stock kind of spread around town so we don't have to spend so much on overhead."

"Oh, I didn't know how it worked. I hoped you'd have something I could use this weekend."

"How much did you bring with you?"

Bob reached into his pocket and pulled out two twenties, a ten and some change. "I've got fifty with me," he said hopefully. "And I get paid again on the 15th."

"Fender will cost you four bills," Al answered. "And we don't have a lay away plan. Music store might, but they'll charge you seven fifty and you'll be too old to play by the time you own it. Tell you what, I'll take the fifty as a down payment, then see what we have in stock. What time do you close the station tomorrow?"

"We close at ten and it takes me a few minutes to clean up the shop before I can leave."

"You look like an honest boy," Al said with a laugh. "Maybe we can make a deal."

"Thanks," Bob said, not knowing the name of the man he just gave his last dollar to. "See you at ten."

~ ~

When Bob entered the tavern, its smoke and stale-beer smell assaulted his senses.

This is where it all starts, he thought to himself. *All the great ones started out just like this, paying their dues and waiting to get noticed.*

Brad and Carl were already setting up. A third guy was running the cords and setting up the mics.

Carl turned to Bob and asked, "Did ya get the amp?"

"Not yet. He's going to check the stock and meet me tomorrow night."

Carl and Brad looked at each other and began to laugh.

"Well, get your gear and get hooked up," Brad said. "But this is the last time we share my amp. I need all the watts I can get."

~ ~

Bob had grown up in a Christian home with his mother and two sisters. His father had been killed in Desert Storm before Bob was old enough to remember him. Until he had left home the only time he had played to a crowd had been in his church's worship team. When he dropped out of college he moved out of the house and a hundred miles away from the only home he had ever known. He was only a two-hour drive away, but a world apart from family and friends. He was making his own way, his own decisions, and not taking criticism for his dreams.

~ ~

The '64 Econoline ran like new, providing both transportation and shelter when the weather got nasty. He'd rebuilt the engine in high school auto shop and decked it out inside with all the necessities except a shower and toilet. On a regular basis he would work until ten at the station and would return after a gig where he could use the rest room and plug into the outside outlet. His hotplate and mini refrigerator didn't pull enough juice to worry his boss. His old Gibson had been a gift from his grandmother back when he was in middle school.

Bob had only been in town two weeks and was still getting the lay of the land when he met Brad and Carl at a music shop. Although both smoked and drank, Bob had not seen either use drugs. He hoped to distance himself from them and the tavern-style life when he got his big break.

~ ~

"Give me a D," Brad said, tuning his guitar.

Bob obliged, smiling. The deep rich vibrations tingled in his ears. Carl was finishing a gratis drink and began to pick up a beat from somewhere in his head. Their keyboard was Billy, a thirty-something local, who played for drinks and to pick up whatever groupies might be left at closing. He did his own thing and did not answer to either Carl or Brad. He brought his own equipment and left whenever the urge struck him.

Bob's voice was good, but not strong enough to do more than provide harmony for Brad, who enjoyed the limelight. "Joy to the World," the old Jeremiah was a bullfrog song, was their first number.

As they sang, Bob thought how Jeremiah was also a prophet of God.

The tavern closed at two with the drunken crowd taking several minutes to clear out before the doors were locked and cleanup began. The band split the offered sixty dollars, which gave each twenty for the night's work since Billy had left early with one of the local women. As he pocketed his twenty and helped carry their gear to the cars, Bob began to see his less glamorous service station job in a clearer light.

As Bob approached his old Ford, it became clear to him he had forgotten to lock it up.

"Who's in there?" he questioned as he heard voices and saw movement.

"Just us. Take a walk," Billy answered.

He had found Bob's unlocked van and had taken the liberty of saving the price of a room.

At first Bob was angry, then disillusioned at how life was not what he had expected. As he walked around the empty parking lot he began to miss his home, his family, and his former life. He looked up at the cloudless night sky filled with tiny points of light and imagined the hand of God arranging them perfectly according to His design.

He had gotten out of the habit of praying. Life had pushed it aside since he had left home. But now, Bob felt like he was standing in the great throne room of heaven. He could almost see God on His throne as he prayed with only the starlight to reflect the tears in his eyes.

"God," he said, quietly, "I feel so far from you, so far from home and alone. I am having trouble knowing right from wrong and standing strong in the faith. Please help me."

His prayer was cut short by the slamming of the van's door and Billy calling out, "Hey, Bass Boy, you out there? You can come back now."

When he returned to the van there was a self-important smirk on the Billy's face. Clearly embarrassed, the woman just looked away. Billy was a slight-built man whose ego and mouth made him seem bigger than he was. Bob towered several inches over him.

Bob moved in close and said, "The van is my home. I don't expect you to ever enter my home again without my permission. Is that understood?"

Billy was ten years his senior and was not about to be humiliated in front of his new girlfriend. "Is that so? And just what are you going to do about it?" he asked, moving in close to where the smell of liquor filled Bob's nostrils.

"Lock up my van," Bob said, with a grin and turned to leave.

Billy caught him by the sleeve and attempted to turn him back around, wanting to get in the last word. Bob turned to face him and hit him full force with an open hand in the middle of his chest. The smaller man went over backwards. He hit the pavement on his back with surprise and fear on his face.

Billy got to his feet and opened his mouth to speak, but Bob said, "Leave it alone Billy. I don't like to fight, but I can if need be."

Billy evaporated into the blackness of the night. As he went he threw a couple of coarse remarks over his shoulder.

When Bob got into the van he was overwhelmed with the smell of cigarette smoke and liquor. He wanted badly to be back home, in his own bed, and with his family near him. When he returned to the service station he left the windows of the van open to benefit from the crisp night air. As he lay outside on a folding cot, covered with a blanket, the stars overhead seemed like familiar friends.

When he awoke he found the van stripped and his Gibson gone. Only his clothes remained. *Why? Why me? Why now?* Then he grew angry. At first he was angry at himself for leaving the van open. That anger was quickly transferred to Billy who had made it necessary to air out the van. It was Billy's fault. *I'll make him pay,* he thought. Bob's thoughts were interrupted. His employer had just arrived to open the station.

"Mornin' Bob," Steve said cheerily. "Gonna be a beautiful day. You sleep out under the stars last night?"

"Yeah, I did. And while I was sleeping someone stole all of my gear."

"Sorry to hear that," Steve offered. "I'm not surprised though. We've got a ring workin' around town taking anything that's not tied down. Police know who they are but haven't been able to catch them in the act."

Immediately Bob's thoughts turned to the events of the previous day and of his solicitation of a man who provided from his stock scattered all over the town. His anger turned to shame. It was people like him who made it possible for criminals to stay in business.

"Be sure and report it," Steve advised. "Though it won't do any good unless they catch them."

Bob felt his pocket to make sure he still had his wallet and the twenty dollars from the previous night. He did.

"Thank you, Lord," he said to himself. *At least I can eat today,* he thought as he put the cot and the blanket back into the van.

"You have enough food to get you to payday?" Steve asked. "The missus and I always have extra if you'd like to come by and have dinner with us."

"I'm fine," Bob answered. "They didn't get my wallet, but they took my guitar."

"Shame," Steve said. "I know it was special to you. I'll say a prayer that you get it back."

"Thanks," Bob said appreciatively. "I'll see you tonight."

At the restaurant he wondered if he should get a light-eater breakfast and be hungry before noon or get the grand slam and skip lunch. He was still muddling it over when a policeman came in and sat at the counter beside him. They acknowledged each other with a nod.

"You decided?" the waitress asked.

Bob smiled shyly and said, "Why don't you order for me. I have enough for a good breakfast or lunch but not both."

She smiled and winked. "Slam it. Live for today and let God provide for tomorrow. I think I read that somewhere in the Bible."

The officer smiled. "Sue, I think you have the right idea but the wrong words. It says that God has promised to provide for our needs, but not necessarily our wants. We are supposed to trust that He will provide and not worry about the future." He turned to Bob and said, "How about I buy the breakfast this morning and you save your money for lunch?"

"That's kind of you to offer," Bob said, reddening with embarrassment. It's my own fault, I got no one to blame 'cept myself."

"You working?" the officer asked.

"Yeah, but only part time down at the Exxon station. I was trying my hand with a band but someone stole my guitar last night."

"So you're the guy who works nights for Steve," he said, extending his hand toward Bob. "I'm Blake Meltzer. I saw the van there several nights and stopped and asked Steve about it. He told me about you. You report the theft yet?"

"Nah, been too bummed out about the whole thing to think straight," Bob answered honestly. "You really think it would do any good?"

"Son, that's the reason they get away with it. Good people don't seem to want to get involved and just take their losses. They aren't willing to step up and identify them."

Sue returned with their breakfasts.

"Where are you from?" Officer Meltzer asked between bites.

"Coalville," Bob replied. "Lived there all my life before going off to college."

"This is no college town," Officer Meltzer said.

"I dropped out after the second semester. I came here to get closer to Nashville. I thought I had a better chance to get noticed if I was closer."

The officer smiled. "I grew up here, played music all of my life, never got the call either. What do you play?"

"Bass," Bob said, enjoying the conversation and the food. "My grandma gave me my grandpa's old Gibson electric."

"Wow. Depending on the model that's worth some real money. You'll never replace it."

"I know. I suppose I didn't give it proper value because it was given to me. It means more to me now that it's gone."

"I hear you there," Officer Meltzer said. "There was a song about that when I was growing up. 'Don't know what you got 'till it's gone, we paved paradise and put up a parking lot,' or something like that."

Both laughed as they finished eating. The officer paid the bill and gave Sue a tip and a wink.

"When you gettin' married Sue? Some young guy out there is missing the boat."

They walked out together. Bob thanked his new friend for the meal.

"You're welcome. Why don't you follow me down to the station and make out a report?"

Bob hesitated. "It's kind of complicated. I think it's partly my own fault."

The officer looked at him strangely and said, "Tell me about it."

Leaning against the patrol car, Bob began from the time he came to town, telling everything in detail. He even stopped to apologize when he came to the part about looking for the amp, admitting that he suspected the man was less than honest. Officer Meltzer showed special interest when Bob told of the meeting later in the evening at the station.

"Why do you think he would be bringing the amp down for you to see knowing that you don't have the cash to buy it?" Officer Meltzer asked pointedly. "Did you think he had changed his mind and was going to put you on a payment plan?"

"I really hadn't thought about it. He just offered, so I figured he might offer a deal I could afford."

"Oh, he'll offer you a deal all right. It'll be a deal that'll put you right on his payroll, and then he'll own you."

Bob felt fear. "What should I do, just tell him I don't need it anymore since I don't have a guitar?"

"Son," the officer said, "let's go down and visit with my chief. I think he'll have an idea of just what to tell him when he shows up."

Bob followed the patrol car wondering if he should not have told the whole story and if he had gotten into trouble by doing so. He followed Officer Meltzer inside the station and waited while he talked with the chief. Finally he was invited to join them in a private office.

Chief Miller was a tall man with gray hair, looking like a combination of Clint Eastwood and Tommy Lee Jones. He had a serious disposition, but also had smile lines around his mouth. He asked Bob to repeat the story he had just heard from Officer Meltzer.

"You know that someone's been looking out for you don't you?" the chief said, with feeling. "If all these events hadn't happened, you'd have met the man tonight, and then in the near future we'd be arresting you for accepting stolen merchandise - or worse."

Bob could only nod.

"God has put good folks around you to protect you and has made you a part of His plan to give these crooks what they deserve. Doesn't it seem a little odd to you that Officer Meltzer would show up at just the right place and time this morning? Or even that Billy's misuse of your van forced you to leave the van accessible to theft? Many have prayed that these thieves would be brought to justice. Maybe you chose our little town by divine guidance."

Bob was thinking back to his years attending church with his family and studying the Bible with his grandmother and mother. He remembered the sermons that told how God works in mysterious ways to accomplish His will among men. This seemed a long way around the block for God to bring a crook to justice. *Why hadn't He just let them be caught in the act?*

"What should I do?" Bob asked, feeling like a small child.

"The chief and his officer were both smiling.

"This isn't like television. We don't wire you up with a mic and take down the perps when we get them on tape. This is a small town and we operate like a small town," the chief explained. He pulled a 20-year-old cassette recorder from a drawer, set it on his desk and pushed record. The moment he spoke the recorder was activated and recorded their dialogue, which he played back to them.

"It works like a charm, but you have to be in the room with it when you speak. Just set it on a shelf out of sight and talk normally."

"First thing you should do is challenge him. Tell him that you know he stole your Gibson and you want it back. Then wait and see what he has to say," Officer Meltzer said.

"I'm afraid I'll be nervous and he'll be able to tell," Bob said.

The chief smiled. "You should be nervous. He'll expect you to be nervous. You are not a criminal, just a kid in a bad position. You'd be nervous even if you weren't on the right side of this thing."

"As soon as you file the report of the theft of your guitar, you are clean. If he returns it or even admits having it, we have probable cause for a search warrant. If he denies knowledge of the theft, we'll have to wait and see what he has up his sleeve regarding the amp," Officer Meltzer said.

"What if he asks me to do something illegal? What do I do then?" Bob asked.

"You'll have to use good judgment to avoid breaking the law or causing entrapment. Best advice I can offer is that you cannot be actively involved in a crime. You must stay passive or appear to be an observer," the chief said.

"You can let something happen, but you cannot cause it to happen," Officer Meltzer clarified. "We'll be watching, but we do not have resources to listen in like they do in larger jurisdictions. We'll be relying on you to give us a signal if you want us to come in."

"How will I signal you?" Bob asked.

"What is your normal procedure after closing?" Officer Meltzer asked.

"I turn out the outside lights, shut off the pumps, lock the doors, put the money in the floor safe, and clean the lube bay and rest rooms. Then I turn out the rest of the lights and leave." Bob answered.

"If you turn the outside lights on a second time, we'll come in," the chief said. "If you follow your normal procedure, we'll wait until he leaves before coming in."

~ ~

Bob arrived at work a few minutes early and was greeted by Steve, who was eager to get home to a hot meal. He gave Bob a few last minute instructions before passing him the keys and lightening the till into the safe. A battery was on the charger awaiting pick up, the windows needed washing, and there was a flat tire waiting to be fixed and balanced. Even so, the evening dragged by slowly. At eight fifteen he installed the battery, collected the fee, and finished washing windows. As he finished sweeping, mopping, and emptying the garbage from the lube bay someone arrived wanting an oil change. *Isn't that always the way, he thought. You have 3,000 miles to plan it and you wait until nine o'clock to make it an urgent matter.* The oil change only took fifteen minutes. It did, however, take his mind off the pending rendezvous. Around nine thirty he checked the rest rooms and found one toilet stopped up and water on the floor. He pulled out the snake and mop bucket to clean it all up. It was just ten o'clock when he finished and turned out the restroom lights. He returned to the front, locked the doors, and turned off the outside lights. He then put the bills through the drop slot in the floor and hid the change tray in the back room. He nearly forgot to activate the recorder but did so just as a van pulled into the drive-through and turned out its lights.

Bob took a deep breath. For the sake of the recorder he said, "Here we go. He's here."

A knock on the door gave him a start. From inside the lube bay the office lights made the windows seem like mirrors. It occurred to Bob that he didn't even know the man's name. He unlocked the door and allowed him to enter.

"Well, Bob," the man said with a smirk, "here we are again. I've been watchin' you. You're a hard worker. You ready to deal?"

"You know I'm not," Bob said indignantly. "You stole my Gibson and I want it back."

"Don't go getting all excited now, Bobby," the older man said. "We just took it to show you we can get anything we want, anytime."

"So let's have it before we go any further," Bob said.

"Hold on now, kid. Watch your mouth, or you may never see it again."

Bob took a deep breath. "Do you have it with you?"

"Sho'nuff, right out in the van with your new amp," he said. "Wanna come out and see them?"

"You bring the Gibson in first," Bob said, fearing he might lose the audio recording. "Then we can discuss the amp. That guitar belonged to my grandpa."

"I wondered why you were so steamed. It was just a little joke among friends. You sleeping like a baby only ten feet away while we cleaned you out."

"We are not friends," Bob said. "I don't even know your name."

"Call me Al. Now are we friends?"

"Yeah, Al, we're friends as soon as I get my hands on my guitar," Bob answered sarcastically.

Al went out the door without speaking. As he did, Bob saw a weapon outlined in the fabric of his jacket. When he returned he was carrying the Gibson and was accompanied by a second and third man.

Bob took the guitar case and opened it to check on its contents. "Who are these men, Al? What are they doing here?"

"These are my brothers, Bob. I asked them along in case you didn't like the deal I am going to offer you on the amp."

"What's that supposed to mean?"

"It means, kid, that one way or the other the deal is going down."

"You know I have no money," Bob argued. "Nowhere near enough to pay the kind of cash you want. I'd sell my van to get you the money, but I need it for for transportation."

"Keep the van. What I want is your set of keys to the station for a few minutes. Then you take the amp and be on your way."

"I can't do that," Bob argued. "Steve trusts me."

"Old Steve has insurance. He'll be back in business in no time. You can either give them to us or we will take the Gibson and the keys." He raised his jacket to show Bob the gun.

Bob's heart turned cold with fear, but he spoke with authority. "I can't do it. It'd be traced back to me. How about if I left the front door unlocked? An honest mistake anyone could make and I'd have time to run down the street and have a bite to eat with plenty of witnesses to vouch for me."

Al smiled wickedly. "Splendid idea. I knew you were a smart kid." He turned to the others and said, "Put the amp in his van and then pull around back while he turns out the lights and leaves."

Bob was trying to think fast. If he turned out all of the lights and left the station, would the police know to wait and watch or should he signal and have them come in before they began the thefts?

He was still trying to decide when Al spoke again. "There's been another change of plans," he said. "I think I want to keep the amp and the

Gibson and make you a hero for trying to stop a burglary." He took out the gun and said, "Shut out the lights."

The chief sat in his unmarked car with Officer Meltzer and watched the events unfold. When the two additional men joined the first in the station, Officer Meltzer was ready to call it all off to protect Bob. But the chief's decision prevailed, and they sat watching while the two men left to pull their van behind the building. They both thought they saw the man inside pull a weapon just before he and Bob went into the lube bay. The office lights went out along with the lights in the lube bay. Bob then turned on the canopy lights. He turned the canopy light back off again, leaving only the minimal nightlights on inside.

"What's with the lights?" asked the two men returning from their van.

"Dang kid hit the wrong switch," Al said in an irritated voice. "Roll the big door up and bring the van inside where we can load it out of sight." Al waved the gun at Bob. "Come on, show me the money." They walked back into the office where Bob explained that the money was in the floor safe and he didn't have the combination.

"SOP, it's just like a boss," Al said. "Save the money, and let the employees take the heat."

The door was up and the black van was slowly backing in when Officer Meltzer and the chief slipped in unseen.

"Police! Drop the gun! Don't make me shoot you," Officer Meltzer said, illuminating the room with his mag light. His weapon was trained on Al.

"Down on the floor," the chief said to the two out in the bay. He jacked a shell into his 12-gauge for effect.

"Live to fight another day. I wasn't going to hurt the kid anyway. He's helping us. He's our inside man."

~ ~

Bob stayed in town for three weeks serving as a material witness for the prosecution. Before returning home to his family the little town presented him with a token gift of their appreciation, a new Fender amplifier. All three brothers were convicted on multiple charges. Al had attempted murder added to his list.

For the time being it seemed God's purpose had been fulfilled in the unlikely personage of Bob Smith, who returned to college to pursue a degree in education.

Default Line

He opened his eyes to darkness with the click, click, click of the wheels and the vibration and movement of his environment suggesting that he was aboard a train. With the blinds on the windows closed, he had no idea if it was day or night or how long he had been asleep. Interestingly, he could not remember details of why or to where he was traveling.

He arose from the confines of the small room and found the latch to the window covering and released it. The powdery blackness was replaced by a grayness that revealed more distinctly the appointments of his domain. Through the window he saw outlines of never-ending scenery that remained indistinct in the moonlight. Trees, conifers by their shape, moved by like pickets on a fence in their monotony with only an occasional break between them to establish their individuality. In the distance the silhouettes of mountains met the darkened sky, showing only a slight contrast.

The radium dial on his watch glowed eerily when displaying the time at a few minutes after three o'clock. Jason felt rested but at the same time was drawn to return to the cocoon of his bed knowing that much of the night still remained. His head had barely hit the pillow when sleep embraced him in its arms and took him to a faraway land.

When he awoke a second time light from outside poured into the room. A glance told him that day had replaced night but had done little to alter the scenery visible through the glass. It was obvious to him that the terrain could accurately be described as forested high mountains. The dark green needles of the pine forest were only occasionally broken by a small stand of fir, which sported a more silver shade of color. The highest of the distant mountains remained snowcapped while the closer vistas spoke of late spring or early summer.

Although fitted with a pair of bunk beds, he was the sole occupant of the small traveling compartment. A small interior door led him to a bathroom cubicle, hardly larger than those on an aircraft, but sufficient for his current needs. He washed his face and hands, ran his fingers through his blond hair, and straightened his clothes while looking into the small mirror. A dull hum was accompanied by the sound of the train's steel wheels clicking their way across the joints of the rails. The vibration and slight sideways roll filled his senses as he opened the door into a hallway. To his left the hall ended at a door, which he presumed led to the adjoining car. To his right was a corridor with many small doors just like his own and at its end another door led toward the front of the train.

There were several windows along the hallway facing outward. They exhibited similar scenery to that which he had viewed from his own window on the other side. He walked with his feet apart, much like a sailor on a ship, adjusting for the movement of the train and maintaining his balance as he moved toward the door. Opening the door he noticed a landing, which bridged the few feet between the cars. It was protected from the weather by a slanted overhang that neatly covered the expanse.

As he opened the door to the next car, he observed a very diverse cross section of humanity seated along both sides of the compartment with a walkway down the center. Most of the seats were side by side,

facing another set just like them. A few of the occupants looked up when the door opened but quickly returned their focus to what they had been doing. The car was filled with the noise of multiple conversations. He noticed a woman and a small girl facing forward, with a man and a boy opposite them looking toward the rear of the train. He presumed they were a family. Just as he passed by, the girl knocked over a drink and spilled its contents on the table. Behind him he heard the recriminations of both parents, which were then repeated a second time more loudly for the benefit of those seated nearby. Just beyond them he observed a well-dressed man with a woman half his age sitting beside him. She was laughing at whatever he said. By her dress and makeup he guessed she was his mistress and not his daughter. Still farther toward the back of the car, four poorly dressed young men stared at him with defiant looks in their eyes.

He made note that every seat was filled, leaving him no place to sit even if he had desired to do so. Continuing on he exited the car. As the door closed behind him the barnyard gaggle was silent but began anew as he opened the door to the next car.

As he stepped into the car the scene repeated itself exactly. He saw the same family of four, the well-dressed man and woman, and the young men. He quickly made his way through the car to get to the next one. This occurred again and again. His mind was having trouble comprehending what his eyes were seeing. Frustrated, he stopped moving and closed his eyes. A vision from his childhood filled his mind. It was the time when his father had taken him to an amusement park and into the hall of mirrors. When he opened his eyes the familiar scenery outside the windows was still moving by and the sounds and movement of the train continued unabated. As he turned to retrace his steps toward his berth, the car was dark, and no passengers were visible. The sounds of the passengers' senseless chatter had disappeared. Only the light from outside allowed him to find his way.

"Oh, God," he said out loud, "what is going on? Am I losing my mind?"

The only answer to his questions was the click, click, click of the iron wheels on the rails beneath him.

He walked the length of the car and opened the door leading to the next, expecting to find another like itself. Instead, the door opened into the car with the long hallway and the doors to the sleeping berths. He longed to return to his own cabin to close his eyes and sleep. He wanted to put the nightmare behind him. As he tried one door after another, all were locked. When he neared the front of the car, the exit door opened and the conductor appeared before him.

"I, I don't have a ticket," he said, feeling in his pockets feverishly. "Where am I? What train is this? Where is it going?"

The conductor smiled and said, "Don't worry about a ticket. You paid the fare years ago. You are aboard the Default Line. Anyone who did not choose the other will end up here. I'm sure you know where it is going."

He ran past the conductor to the door. It opened into darkness. No engine or other cars were connected to it. Beneath him the ground stood still, but on both sides the scenery repeated itself over and over again as if in a cartoon. The sound of the wheels and movement of the car were manufactured and electronically produced.

He turned back and ran to the conductor in a panic. "I didn't choose to be here."

Again the conductor smiled and said, "To refuse to ride on the Grace Line is to choose the Default Line."

Deception

Only God has true and complete insight into the heart and mind of man. It is truly rare for the rest of us to get anything more than a superficial look into someone else's soul.

~ ~

"You're kidding," Chip said. "I had lunch with him yesterday. He seemed normal to me. He was telling me about his plans to break away and start up his own company."

"No, I'm not kidding," the caller replied. "We just got word of it from his supervisor."

"Such a shame," Chip said. He has a family doesn't he?"

"Yeah, a wife and two children still at home. He was only thirty-two."

"Thirty-two? He seemed older to me. I'd have guessed closer to forty. But then I didn't know him well. We just attended the same church," Chip mused.

~ ~

"What's good?" he asked, "This is my first time here."

"I always order breakfast," Chip said, "because I like breakfast no matter what time I come in. I've heard the French dip and the Reuben are killer too."

"Reuben then," he said, smiling. "I like the blend of the sweet and sour and the texture of the rye bread."

"You sound like something off the Cooking Channel. Do you always analyze your food that way?"

"I'm an engineer," he answered. "I'm told that we are an unusual breed and that our minds are wired differently than regular folk."

They shared a laugh just as the waitress arrived to take their orders.

"So, you are an engineer. What kind of engineer?"

"Electrical, mostly computer stuff. I design and troubleshoot new products."

"How do you like it?"

"Love it! It's almost like being an artist who can create whatever he likes and still gets a paycheck."

"Wished I could say the same," Chip said sadly. "After all these years, my job has begun to lose its appeal."

"Maybe God is guiding you in another direction. Maybe there's something else out there that He wants you to do."

"Maybe, but at my age it gets pretty scary quitting the only thing you have ever done and starting all over."

"I'm not saying you should; only that you should keep an open mind to it if it comes your way. I've considered quitting and starting my own company."

"But you just told me you loved your job," Chip said.

"The job yes, not necessarily the company. Their focus is on the bottom line with little consideration to morality or the consequences of their decisions to their staff or customers."

Chip nodded as he filled his mouth with scrambled eggs and sausage. "That seems to be the way of the world today," he said.

"Sadly, you are right. The way of the world is the key phrase. I'd like to do what I do, make a fair living, and follow God's leading, not the balance sheet. Thank you for inviting me to Bible study. I've enjoyed the study, meeting the men, and getting to know them."

"They are a good bunch," Chip said. "We try to provide support for each other when hard times come."

~ ~

The phone rang five times with no answer. It was the fourth time in the last hour he had dialed without success but had chosen not to leave a message. His cheeks were wet with tears, and his hands shook as he placed the cell phone on the kitchen counter. He shuddered as he took a deep breath in an attempt to calm himself. The house was quiet, too quiet. He could hear the sound of the second hand on the quartz clock as it methodically completed orbit after orbit around the perimeter of its face.

His mind was filled with the impossibility of his situation, leaving no room for analysis or possible solution. It was like a light switch had been thrown, turning daylight into darkness. Charges of sexual misconduct had been brought against him by one of his staff and were being moved on as though he were guilty. He had been given no opportunity to refute the charges. He had been placed on administrative leave without pay and escorted from the building. They even took away his access card. His head was still swimming with the reality of the telephone conversation with his wife.

"When were you going to tell me?" she said. "How long has it been going on?"

"Barb," he began, but his voice failed him. "Let me explain."

"There's nothing to explain now. It's too late," she said cutting him off.

"But it is not true. Nothing you have heard is true."

But it was too late. The dial tone replaced her voice before his last sentence could be heard.

How had she heard so quickly, he thought. *What had she heard? Why had she been so eager to believe the lie and not give him an opportunity to set the record straight?* He tried to call her back without success. What should he do now? Who could help him straighten it all out? As he reflected back on how it all started he was overcome with a feeling of hopelessness and despair.

~ ~

"You have been coming to work late, abusing your break time, and often leave work early making others pick up the slack," he had said as they sat in a private area of a small cafe near the plant.

He had chosen to give her the opportunity to hear and respond to his job evaluation in a more relaxed setting, away from prying ears.

"In all fairness I should be recommending you for dismissal," he continued. "But I wanted to hear your side of the story and see if we can work it out first."

He had hoped that she would take the opportunity to clean up her act, that she would acknowledge her failings, and ask for another chance. He hated this part of his job because he was ill-suited to deny mercy when he knew that he had received mercy.

She looked at him coldly. "You've never liked me have you?" she accused. "You've never really given me a chance. You have your favorites, and that's just the way it is."

He was shocked at her attack. For several seconds he had no reply. "That is untrue," he said. "I do not dislike you ..."

She stood up quickly and turned to leave. "You haven't heard the last of this," she said, over her shoulder.

As the door closed behind her, he sat there shaking his head. *She just didn't get it,* he thought.

It had been a mistake to try and resolve the issue without an official reprimand in the workplace.

Later that afternoon he was summoned into the supervisor's office. The HR man, corporate attorney and COO were already seated.

"Some serious charges have been brought against you," Mr. Parker from HR began. "There are accusations of a sexual nature, which will not be tolerated."

He could not believe what he was hearing. For a second he thought it was a joke, but knew the presence of the COO precluded that possibility. Then, her last words rang in his ears, *"You haven't heard the last of this."* He knew Peggy had not only intended to punish him for the evaluation but to attack his credibility as well. A woman's scorn was the phrase he had heard but never personally experienced…until now.

"This is a misunderstanding ..." he began, expecting an opportunity to explain his position.

"You'll have your chance to defend yourself after we have completed a thorough internal investigation of your conduct," the attorney interrupted. "Beginning now you are on leave without pay. You'll be asked to surrender your ID badge and escorted from the building by security."

"Don't I have the right to face my accuser?" he asked, feeling anger surface in his voice.

"In due time, in due time," the barrister said. "But remember you are not the injured party here."

Injured party? he thought to himself. *Yes, I am. I am the one who is being punished for an unfounded accusation from a bad employee without consideration of the facts.*

"Travis, listen. Won't you even allow me to tell my side of the story?"

"I'm sorry, I can't. Not at this juncture," Travis said.

~ ~

"What's that about?" Megan asked, referring to the meeting in the supervisor's office.

"I heard he has something going on with Peggy," Cathy answered. "Apparently, she took it upstairs."

"I wonder if Barb knows yet," Megan responded. "Such a shame, they've got two small kids."

~ ~

This is how the conversations started at all levels. Peggy remained on the job. While she feigned reluctance she actually relished the opportunity to provide the juicy but fallacious details. Someone took the liberty to report the stories to Barb and the kids They justified their actions by saying they were only trying to protect them. Satan had a busy and profitable day, crippling and destroying one of God's children while plying the tools of his trade through human weakness.

~~

It was the normal practice of the Bible study group to visit for a few minutes while latecomers arrived. It gave them a chance to grab coffee and discuss the recent events in each person's life before digging into God's Word. When they had all arrived and quieted their conversations, Chip stood and shared the story of their brother who had recently taken his life. He included the information that had just come to light that established his innocence. He then asked that they each remember his wife and children in their prayers.

Small Minded

Often, but not always, a person's stature reflects more about them than their size. And too, their carriage and deportment speak volumes about their sense of self.

~ ~

Nathan was a small boy, just a shade over five feet. Even in 1960, when the population revered a man approaching six feet, he was more comfortable among throngs of women than men. Not that he was effeminate; hardly so, he was every bit a man, just small.

Nathan had fallen behind his peers at about age twelve when the summer sun had seemed to cause many of them to sprout like stalks of corn in the field. Returning to school that fall, he was inches shorter than most in the sixth grade class.

In sports and physical activities he always seemed to be half a step behind his friends. In the beginning his quickness and agility made up some of the difference. But later, when their coordination caught up with their bodies, he found himself left in the dust. That is about the time when he redirected his efforts to the more academic aspects of life.

Nathan's father, a brick mason, was not tall, about five feet five inches. His sturdy frame and massive muscles, the result of years of hard

labor, made him seem taller than he actually was. His mother, a schoolteacher and pianist, took pride in her son's newfound interest in academia. He even has her teach him how to play the piano. His father, however, never missed an opportunity to work his lack of size into a conversation. To Nathan it left a wound that became an open sore that separated them and pushed him all the more toward his mother.

Like many fathers, it was Nathan's father's hope that his son would follow in his footsteps. He wanted him to learn the trade and someday take over the family business. They attended a small community church each week, enjoying the social interaction. When the pastor asked Nathan to play the piano before the congregation, his father feigned illness and stayed home. Nathan supposed his father was too humiliated to endure his peer's remarks.

It became a wedge that grew larger as time went by; a barrier that was never discussed, an unresolved issue. The more his mother attempted to compensate, the more noticeable the rift became between them. The final straw came when Nathan was in high school and took a job working at the music store.

~ ~

At the age of nineteen Nathan reached five feet six inches. He was a full inch taller than his father, but weighed only 124 pounds. He took pride in joining the Army. He volunteered for service in Vietnam rather than waiting, as many had, for the draft to catch up with them. For a time it seemed that he and his father might be reconciled. He had hoped his father would approve of his new military status.

After thirteen weeks of boot camp and special training to prepare him for battle, Nathan took his place among the young and courageous. Surrounded by men of every ethnic, physical and geographic representation, he felt more at home than he had in years. The camaraderie they shared made the ribbing they showered on one another not offensive, but unifying. The discerning eyes of the veteran leaders seemed godlike in their ability to discover the gifts each man brought to the table. Their special abilities were quickly capitalized upon as each man was assigned to a position matched to their unique skills.

Nathan, nicknamed "The Weasel," was a quick study when trained in close combat. Quick, strong and agile, he was selected to explore the many tunnels the Viet Cong dug in the jungles. Most often he'd find a cache of weapons, explosives or food that needed to be destroyed, but occasionally he was forced to dispatch its occupants with a single knife thrust. During times like this many soldiers walked a precarious personal line between pursuing life or death. Nathan found himself moving closer and closer to God. One of the Ten Commandments, "You shall not kill," haunted him. He had already killed several times and didn't quite know how to handle it. With Satan's help the issue grew and grew in his mind, making him question his own convictions.

~ ~

During a seven-day R&R in the area known as the "Secure Zone," Nathan sought out the company chaplain and laid out his feelings. Captain Miller was the right man for the job. Gifted by God and chosen by man, he offered spiritual insights to those men who faced death daily and so badly needed help. Miller was first and foremost a good listener. He was also astute at reading between the lines of sentences half-vocalized. Often he found what was described as the problem was not the problem at all, but simply a symptom of the real issue. Nathan found him a safe haven, a mentor, a counselor, and a father figure.

"I believe that the original Hebrew language makes a distinction between murder and killing. I say that knowing both God and man killed their enemies in large numbers throughout the Old Testament," Miller explained.

Nathan nodded.

"I say that not from personal experience but from my own belief in the true goodness of God. God loves His creation, all of them. It makes no sense that He would say, 'You shall not kill,' and then kill them Himself. He never contradicts Himself."

"I view murder as killing without cause or for personal gain. I see killing as sometimes a necessary part of life in this cruel world," Nathan replied.

Miller smiled and nodded his agreement. "Couldn't have said it better myself. So what is your concern?"

"Mostly I just wanted to have a second opinion. It seems to me that we can fool ourselves into believing anything we want if we aren't careful."

"You are correct there. That is why God calls us to stay in the company of other believers. We all need support and sometimes a good slap alongside the head to get our thinking right."

Nathan smiled.

"What is really bothering you? What is the burden that you carry and can't lay down?"

Nathan hesitated, unsure if he could put it into words. Tears began forming in his brown eyes and a lump threatened to close off his airway. "My father," he gasped. The words rushed out like a flood. "I think I hate my father."

Miller's face changed. Concern registered in his features. "Would you share with me why you feel this way?"

The floodgates of repressed emotion opened. As Nathan told him the story of his childhood years, he was forced to stop several times and regain control of himself. When he finally stopped talking he felt exhausted. He was drained of emotion but somehow felt cleansed and relieved.

"Are you angry at your father, or are you angry at yourself because you were not able to please him? Is your disappointment in him and the way he treated you or in your inability to tell him how he made you feel?"

Nathan didn't answer right away. He took several minutes to examine the questions he had been asked and objectively consider them. "Both," he finally said. "There was a time when I may have been able to tell him. But that time came and went without the issues being addressed. Then I began to feel resentment. I began to give him all the blame and felt licensed to do things I knew would hurt him."

"Can you forgive him?" Miller asked. "Can you forgive yourself?"

"I don't know. I want to."

"God will not forgive you until you have forgiven others," Miller said softly. "Will you pray with me and ask for His help?"

Nathan nodded.

Miller bowed his head, took the younger man's hand in his and began, "Our Father who art in heaven ..."

Nathan repeated the Lord's prayer after him, stumbling and began to weep when he got to the part "forgive us as we forgive ..."

Captain Miller took it from there, "Father, you made each of us in your image. You delight in your creation. You love us with an unending love. You gave your only Son in our place that we may be forgiven and spend eternity with you. As you have forgiven us, you have commanded that we likewise forgive others. Help us today to accept the pain we have received and to forgive, to repent from the pain we have caused, and to be forgiven. Please remove the burden of guilt from our shoulders and free us from the bondage of sin. Amen."

~ ~

"Dad?" Nathan said into the phone. "Are you there, Dad?"

Nathan's father was roused from sleep. His mind feared what he might hear. "Nathan, is that you? Are you all right?"

"Yes, Dad, it's me. I'm all right. I just wanted to call and tell you I love you. I want to ask you to forgive me for the pain I have caused you over the years."

Seconds went by without a sound.

"I love you too, Son. I always have. I never knew how to show it."

"But, Dad, I have always felt like I disappointed you. I was always small, not the son you wanted me to be."

There was a sound of a choking sob on the other end of the phone. The sound was of a man racked with guilt and pain.

"There are no small men, Son, only small-minded men."

It Is Finished

Tuesday after school Huck did not take to the court but hit the weight room and followed it up with the whirlpool bath. He was still sore from the car accident but walked without a limp. On his way home he picked up his brother, Brent, at the middle school. When they got home their mother had dinner ready.

"Got a 94 percent on the pop quiz yesterday," Brent said, faking a look of disappointment.

"Oh, boohoo. Try harder," Huck said, giving little sympathy.

"Good job," his mother said. "By the way, I spoke to Rose Thomas today. She and Steve would like to go up to the hospital tonight to see their sister. I told her we'd pick them up."

Huck nodded, scooped up their dishes, and put them in the dishwasher before heading off to his room to change his clothes. He was anxious to see how Mary was doing at the hospital. She had  been in a coma since the car accident last week.

~ ~

"Hi Beth. Hi guys. Thanks for the ride," Rose said, as she and Steve got in the car. "We have been promised a check on the Infiniti this week, but nothing on the injuries until we are willing to accept a final settlement."

Rose rode up front with Beth while the three boys shared the back seat.

"How are you feelin'?" Huck asked his friend, Steve. "Are the ribs any better?"

"Some, but they still hurt. You're looking better."

"I did a light workout on the weights, then hit the whirlpool," Huck said. "It helped a lot. You should try it."

Steve smiled. "You're a glutton for punishment."

When they arrived at the hospital, Mr. and Mrs. Thomas were there quietly talking to Mary's doctor. Huck felt a little uncomfortable. Since he was driving when the accident occurred, he wondered if they blamed him for their daughter's condition.

When Mary's parents approached, their demeanor was hard to read. As they got closer Muriel had a faint smile and said, "They say the swelling is going down, but she is still unconscious."

Beth reached out and hugged her.

"We have hope that when her body has healed, she will be able to pull out of the coma." Bud said. "The pastor believes that in God's time she will wake up and wonder what all the fuss is about."

The group made their way to Mary's room. Cuts from the shattered glass still showed on the right side of her face. The left side was unblemished and beautiful as she lay there like Sleeping Beauty waiting for her prince. There was little to do or say as the minutes seemed to endlessly drag on.

"We should pray." Muriel said.

The seven bowed their heads and one by one quietly lifted up their prayers to the One who has the power to heal.

~ ~

Back at home Beth found a few moments alone with Huck. "How's the job?" she asked. "Do you like it at the rehab hospital?

"I really like it. I'm learning a lot about how people relate to each other and to their injuries," Huck answered.

"Sounds more like psychology than physical therapy to me."

"Of the two we have more to do with helping heal the body than the mind." Huck said, proudly, "but God heals them both."

"I'm glad you like it," she replied.

Before going to bed, Beth watched the late news. The meteorologist predicted snow flurries and freezing temperatures. This made her worry about her son's drive to school the next day.

In the morning there was a dusting of snow on the ground with promise of more to come. At breakfast she tried to encourage both boys to take the bus. Huck countered with his need to stay for basketball practice and then go to work.

"Well, at least get some rock salt to put in the trunk. It's good for weight and traction. Stop at the grocery store and pick up a few bags on your way to work. We'll get snow tires this weekend."

Huck used his second-gear trick to get out of the driveway and onto the street where he nursed the Mustang forward by riding the clutch in the higher gear. In spite of the cold, Huck began to sweat as anxiety elevated his body temperature. Since the accident he found it impossible to relax while driving. Brent was nearly late for school and Huck was late by the time he parked and turned off the old Ford.

During fifth period he received a message that his mother had called. She would be picking Brent up after school and she wanted to remind him to purchase the rock salt.

Huck was surprised when he arrived at the gym and saw that Steve was already dressing down. Both boys sported nasty looking black, yellow and blue bruises they received in the accident. On the court they were chided by their teammates as they gimped around the gym.

While the whirlpool was inviting, Huck's need to get to work on time took precedence. En route he also needed to stop by the store to get the rock salt.

When he arrived at work he was greeted by Carol, his co-worker. Carol's son Jerry was on Huck's basketball team at school. On the way to the patients' rooms they visited about the car accident and about how unpredictable life is.

"I prayed that the basketball team would be able to get the win without me." Huck told her.

She laughed. "You think Jesus cares much about which team wins any particular game? I mean with everyone prayin' and all, ain't no way He's gonna please everyone."

Huck had never considered that for some prayers to be granted it might appear that other people's prayers had been denied. Luckily God, and not man, made the decisions that would ultimately determine the outcome.

"Huck, I've been hoping you'd come," Ron said. "I've missed visiting with you lately."

"I'll leave you two alone to visit for a bit while I check on Vi," Carol said.

"I wanted to tell you about the rehab," Ron said, excitedly. "Look."

Ron smiled as he slowly squeezed a tennis ball with his left hand. "I'll be throwing to first base before you know it," he said.

Huck silently offered up a prayer of gratitude. "Wow, you're doing well."

"I can't stand yet, but I can move my toes and feet a bit."

Out of nowhere Huck asked Ron, "Do you believe in Jesus?"

A cloud came over Ron's countenance. "Used to," he said.

"You mean you don't anymore? What changed your mind?"

"Why don't you give me a few minutes alone." Ron said, ignoring the question.

Huck left the room wondering what pain had caused his friend to move away from his faith. He was still standing in the hallway when Carol came out of Vi's room and approached him.

"What's on your mind, Huck?"

"I asked Ron about Jesus and he just clammed up. He asked me to leave."

"I know," she said. "I've tried to talk to him too but something inside just shuts him down. Maybe you should leave it alone."

"I can't," Huck said, with determination. "You can't have secrets between friends."

Carol nodded respectfully. "You are right. Just take it slow and easy."

When Huck returned to the room he respected Ron's desire for privacy. He busied himself by doing some cleanup work.

Looking away from Huck, Ron spoke softly. "Pete was my twin brother, born six minutes before me. He never let me forget it. We both got our chance in the majors, but he was always better than me. He was faster and hit better too. He played second base and batted cleanup. It stinks having a twin brother who is better than you at everything he tries.

The year I quit to join the Army, he was hitting .400, already had 94 RBIs, would have been a shoo-in for MVP. He won the golden glove in his first year."

"What happened?" Huck asked.

"He joined the Army too, but only because I did first. He said he couldn't let his younger brother get one over on him."

"Were you together?" Huck asked. "I mean did you serve together in the same unit?"

"We did. The recruiter made us a special deal. He let us join on the buddy system. They got a lot of mileage out of the fact that two major-leaguers would give it all up to serve their country. They used us as poster boys to encourage others to join."

"Then what happened?" Huck asked.

"After they got all the mileage they could get out of it, they began treating us like everyone else. We were assigned to a recon unit and spent a lot of time in the bush."

Ron talked for a long time, reliving events and places, harrowing and humorous circumstances. He stopped, looked Huck right in the eyes, and said, "Pete died in my arms, took a shot to the throat." Tears rimmed his eyes as the moment became real and painful once again.

Several silent moments went by before he spoke again. "I prayed with all of my heart, offered my life for his, called on Jesus for His mercy and grace, but He did not hear me," Ron said bitterly.

Huck was wise enough to know that he could not argue with a 35-year-old knife through the heart. This wound had been left untreated.

"I don't claim to know what you are feeling, but I lost someone close to me too. My girlfriend died two years ago from cancer," Huck said. "I never chose to tell her that I had fallen in love with her. It hurt so bad. For a while I blamed God for not giving us more time together. Later I realized that Jesus will give us eternity together."

"What was her name?" Ron asked.

"Sara."

"Had you been together long?"

"No. We met at youth group and knew each other for about a year, but it felt longer. We could really communicate. She told me something once that made a real difference at how I look at things. She said she wondered how many times God got blamed for our bad choices, and how many times He wished He could force His will on us. Of course, He loves us too much to force us to live without the freedom to make our own choices."

Ron continued to listen.

"Just a week ago my friends and I were in a car accident. Our friend Mary got hurt really bad and is in a coma. Sara would have said that it wasn't God who caused it, but He did let it happen."

"Couldn't He have stopped you guys from going out driving that night?" Ron asked.

"Yes, but it was Sara's belief that although He guides and directs us, He seldom forces His will on us. We take the credit when things go right and give God the blame when they don't."

Carol entered the room smiling. "How's it going boys?"

"Peachy," Ron said, grinning. "The boy here is teaching me theology."

"Well," she said, "I hope he can finish up soon because it is snowing outside and he should probably head home before it gets worse. You boys can visit again tomorrow."

~ ~

It was ten thirty when he pulled the old "Stang" into the driveway. Huck was glad he had listened to his mother's advice and got extra weight over the drive tires.

"That you Huck?" his mother asked, when she heard the back door close. "Did you have any problems?"

"Nope, no problems. There's hardly anyone on the streets."

"Did you have a good day at work?"

"I did. I spent most of my time talking to an older guy who had a stroke. He was in Vietnam, and his twin brother died in his arms. He has blamed God all of these years."

Beth looked at her son with a new regard. "None of us here at home have any idea of what it was really like over there."

Huck told her about their conversation.

Having overheard their discussion, his brother came into the room smiling. "I have his brother's rookie card," he said. "Peter Kincaid only played two years. They expected him to be another Ted Williams."

Huck took the plastic coated card and looked at it. He could see the resemblance to the old man at the rehab hospital. "How much is this worth? I want to buy it from you."

"You can just have it," Brent said. "You couldn't afford it."

"No seriously, I want to buy it. What's a fair price?"

"I'll look it up on eBay."

"Would you look up Ron Kincaid too?" Huck said. "I want them both."

"I'll see if his card's for sale."

Within a few minutes Brent had the information pulled up on his laptop. "A guy in Spokane has the pair. He's asking $150 for Peter and $125 for Ron. He says he'll sell them as a set and ship them for $250."

"Tell him I'll take them both," Huck said.

~ ~

Thursday morning was blustery and cold. The Mustang had a heavy coat of ice and snow on all of the windows. The snow had stopped falling after delivering a couple more inches, a total now of well over six. Huck rose early, took time to shovel the sidewalk, and let the car warm up. He and Brent left early for school.

The school day went by quickly. Before he knew it, he and Steve were in the gym, getting themselves ready for the game on Friday. When the coach asked Huck how he felt, Huck made the excuse that he was not back to a hundred percent. Huck suggested he play off guard and allow Jerry to take the point guard position. When the coach agreed, Jerry beamed.

Where did that come from? Huck asked himself. *I don't know, but it sure felt like the right thing to do.*

Huck arrived at work early. Not seeing Carol, he changed and went to Ron's room.

"Evening, Ron. How are you feeling today?"

"Happier than a pig in a slop trough," he said.

Huck noted how energetic Ron looked and acted. "You must have had a good session."

"Indeed I did. I stood for the first time today, with some help of course. You're early."

"I left basketball practice early to get a jump on the drive because of the snow. My car is not the best in snow."

"What do you drive?"

"A '69 Ford Mustang, 351, hardtop," he said with pride.

"Four speed?" Ron asked.

"Yeah, why do you ask?"

"I bought a '67 Firebird 400 convertible before I left for 'Nam. I still have it in the garage," he said. "It hasn't been started in years."

"Wow! That's a real classic."

They visited for a few more minutes before Huck noticed Carol still had not made an entrance.

"I'll be right back. I need to check on something," Huck told Ron.

In the hallway Huck saw a nurse coming out of Vi's room. "Excuse me, do you know if Carol is working today?" he asked her.

"Carol had a heart attack this afternoon and was taken to the hospital. She's in CCU last I heard. I'm Verna. I'll be filling in for her. You must be Huck. She talks about you all the time, like you are family."

Huck found a telephone at the nurse's station and called his mother. "Mom, I need a favor," Huck began. "I need you to make some calls for me." He explained to her what he knew about the situation with Carol and that it was likely her children, Jerry and Lily, would need help with transportation or some food. "Please pray for her, Mom."

Huck hung up and bowed his head. He struck up a conversation with his Lord. When he finished he went back into Ron's room.

"Thought you forgot about me," Ron said.

"Sorry, Ron. I found out that Carol was taken to the hospital this afternoon. I called my mom and asked her to try to get hold of her son. He and I go to the same school and play basketball together."

"Will she be all right?"

"I don't know. I pray she will," Huck said. "It's up to God."

"I've given considerable thought to our last conversation when you asked me about Jesus. Have you ever heard the story about the broken rope?" Ron asked.

"No, tell me about it."

Ron smiled. "Once there were two friends. They were as different as night and day. One of them was a country boy, poorly dressed, and poorly educated. The other was a city boy from a fine home who had attended the best of schools. The city boy always dressed in the finest and most up-to-date fashion regardless of where they went or what they did. The other wore work clothes that often needed repair or laundering. One day when they had been out fishing together it began to rain. Soon the stream became swollen with the runoff. When they started home the mud in the roadway caused the city boy to be concerned about his new shoes and fancy clothes. The country boy agreed to carry him on his back. They were nearly home when they heard a noise just off the road. It was the sound of an animal whimpering from a sinkhole. They went to the hole and looked in. They saw a wet and frightened puppy down at the bottom in the mud and water. Without hesitation the country boy unwrapped the rope that he used as a belt, and handed it to his friend. 'Just hold on to the rope and let me down slowly. When I get a hold of the puppy, pull me up,' he instructed. Things went as expected until he neared the bottom. The end of the worn out rope broke and the country boy dropped to the bottom. The city boy was left holding the shortened length of rope in his hands. Its end dangled just out of the reach of his friend. *What shall I do?* he thought. Then without any concern for himself, he dropped to his knees in the muck. His shoes and clothes got caked with mud. He let the rope down to where his friend could grasp the end. They were all smiles as they walked home together, dirty but happy with the shivering puppy in their arms.

"What do you make of that?" Ron asked.

Huck hesitated, thinking through the events of the tale with their possible meanings and interpretations. "Sometimes you have to get down and dirty for a friend!" he said.

"Exactly! You got it my friend. I'm the one who has missed a great deal all of these years. Thank you for taking the chance of damaging our friendship for something much more important."

~ ~

It was just after ten when Huck pulled up outside his house. He announced himself as he came through the back door. The living room was filled with people. Jerry, Lily, Pastor Freeman, Steve and the rest of the Thomas family, and most of the basketball team were all there.

"Come on in," his mother said.

"Is Carol doing better?" Huck asked, hopefully.

"We don't know, but we have faith in God."

Several times over the next hour the group joined together in prayer, lifting up their requests for Carol's healing to the Lord of Lords. Just before midnight the group began wandering off to their homes. Jerry and Lily stayed over in case they needed to get to the hospital.

~ ~

Friday morning came, cold but clear. Beth got up early and had breakfast ready for everyone before they left for school.

"It's awfully nice of you to let us stay over," Jerry said.

The Mustang was full with Brent and Lily in the back and Jerry riding shotgun. The two youngsters were dropped off at the middle school before the boys cautiously made their way to the high school. As with every game day, the halls had been adorned with streamers and students were dressed in their school colors in an effort to promote school spirit.

During lunch time Jerry used a telephone in the counselor's office to call the hospital for an update on his mother. The nurse's station had very little information for him. They did say that she was undergoing a procedure to evaluate the cause of the heart attack. He called again before the final school bell rang. He was put right through to his mother's room where a nurse picked up the phone.

"She's in recovery right now, but the doctor is close by. Give me a minute and I'll let you talk with him," she offered.

"It's called A-fib," the doctor said. "The top half of the heart is operating at a different speed than the lower half causing it to get out of sync. We don't see any long-term damage at this point and will prescribe medication to help her avoid a reoccurrence."

"Can I see her?" Jerry asked.

"Yes, she can have visitors. She told me to tell you to take care of business on the basketball court first, then you can come on up."

Jerry repeated the message to some of his team members who were standing nearby and said, "Sounds like Mom."

And he did just as she instructed. He led the team in points scored for the second straight game, with Huck and Steve combining for an additional thirty-two. They won the game and then Jerry came up to the hospital to visit his mom.

YOU MIGHT ALSO BE INTERESTED IN...

Heaven Help Us

Short Stories Volume Two

AND

Available in print form and Apple & Android applications Find them at

www.prayerfulpublishing.com

www.ingramcontent.com/pod-product-compliance
Lightning Source LLC
Chambersburg PA
CBHW071459040426
42444CB00008B/1406